THE ESSENTIAL TITO

THE ESSENTIAL TITO

Edited with an Introduction by
HENRY M. CHRISTMAN

ST. MARTIN'S PRESS
New York

949.702
T621

AFFILIATED PUBLISHERS: Macmillan & Company, Limited,
London—also at Bombay, Calcutta, Madras and Melbourne—
The Macmillan Company of Canada, Limited, Toronto.

Contents

Introduction by the Editor   vii

The Tasks Before the People's Liberation
   Partisan Detachments   2

At the First Session of the Anti-Fascist
   Council of People's Liberation   8

At the Second Session of the Anti-Fascist
   Council of People's Liberation   14

At the Third Session of the Anti-Fascist
   Council of People's Liberation   34

17485

To the Fifth Congress of the Communist Party
   of Yugoslavia   50

On Workers' Management in Economic Enterprises   78

To the United Nations General Assembly   92

To the Belgrade Conference of Nonaligned
   Countries   122

On Current International and Domestic Issues   152

The Twenty-fifth Anniversary of The New
   Yugoslavia   170

Index   193

Introduction

New Yugoslavia is now a quarter-century old. The Socialist Federal Republic of Yugoslavia is headed by the founder of the state, Josip Broz Tito, a remarkable man who first led a successful military campaign that was both a national resistance movement and a dynamic social revolution, then forged a completely new state with a unique social and economic system.

History, politics, and social developments all have combined to project Tito's Yugoslavia onto the forefront of the world stage. For New Yugoslavia is simultaneously a nation of crucial strategic importance in East-West power politics, a major world example of international nonalignment, and an exciting new social and economic system of vital significance and potential for other nations.

The scope of Tito's achievement is all the more impressive when viewed in historical perspective. Yugoslavia did not even exist as a political entity until 1918. Moreover, this relatively young nation is a land of extraordinary diversity; Yugoslavs like to say that their country is a nation of six republics (Serbia, Croatia, Slovenia, Bosnia-Herzegovina, Macedonia, and Montenegro); five peoples (Serbs, Croats, Slovenes, Macedonians, and Montenegrins); four languages (Serbian, Croatian, Slovenian, and Macedonian); three religions (Eastern Orthodox Christian, Roman Catholic Christian, and Moslem); and two alphabets (Cyrillic and Roman). Even this, however, does not fully express the complexity of modern Yugoslavia, for in addition to the six republics, there are also two autonomous regions—Vojvodina, with a substantial Magyar population of Hungarian culture and language, and Kosovo-Metohija, with a largely Moslem population of Shiptar (Albanian) descent and culture. There are, moreover, at least twelve other distinct minorities, each with its own culture and/or language and/or religion, scattered throughout Yugoslavia.

History has accentuated the distinctive characteristics of each of Yugoslavia's diverse groups. The "Land of the South Slavs" was repeatedly conquered and partitioned by a succession of invaders who plundered the areas under their domination and brutally repressed the subject populations. Yugoslavia was for centuries the battleground of three major cultures and their respective religions: The Austro-Hungarian culture, and Roman Catholicism; Byzantine culture, and Orthodox Christianity; and Ottoman Turkish culture, with the Moslem faith.

For a leader not only to reunite such a diverse nation, but also to direct its transformation into a modern state with a Socialist society and economy, is a remarkable achievement by any standard.

Josip Broz Tito, father of the New Yugoslavia, was born at Kumrovec, near Zagreb, Croatia, then a part of the Austro-Hungarian Empire, on May 25, 1892, of Croat and Slovene parentage. Young Josip Broz served an apprenticeship as a metal worker, then moved to Zagreb, capital of Croatia, where he was drafted into the Austro-Hungarian army upon the outbreak of World War I. Already an activist in the trade union movement and the Social Democratic Party of Croatia, Broz was critical of the war, and spent time in military prison because of his antiwar statements.

Early in 1915, Broz was seriously wounded and taken prisoner by the Russians. He spent more than a year in a hospital in Kazan, then was sent to work in forced labor camps. He escaped several times, and in 1917 took part in the historic July demonstrations in Petrograd. In 1918, after the outbreak of the October Revolution, he joined the Red International Guard. Following the end of World War I, Broz returned to Zagreb and joined the Communist Party of Yugoslavia.

At that time, during the early days of royalist Yugoslavia, the Communist Party was legal; it succeeded in winning 58 of the 419 seats in the Yugoslav Parliament, the Skupština, thus becoming the third largest parliamentary political party. Subsequently, however, the Communist Party was outlawed and driven underground, and even political moderates such as liberals and Social Democrats were banned from public life. Broz then worked as a laborer in various locations in Croatia and Serbia, finally returning to Zagreb. In each of these situations, he agitated on behalf of the workers; he was arrested several times, on one occasion receiving a sentence of five months in prison. Finally, in August, 1928, he was arrested for Communist activities, and in a Zagreb trial which received much publicity, was sentenced to five years of imprisonment.

Upon his release from prison in 1934, Broz again went underground, and began the use of various assumed names, including that of Tito. He rose rapidly in the clandestine Communist hierarchy, becoming Organizational Secretary in 1936, and General Secretary of the Communist Party of Yugoslavia the following year.

Meanwhile, the situation of the royalist government grew steadily worse, and the government responded with intensified repression. The continuing struggle between the Serbs and the other nationalities, particularly the Croats, virtually paralyzed public life throughout Yugoslavia. King Alexander, seeking to strengthen the position of his regime, went to France to confer with French Foreign Minister Louis Barthou. Shortly after his arrival in Marseilles, on October 9, 1934, both men were assassinated. Italian, Hungarian, Bulgarian, and Croatian interests apparently shared responsibility for the murders.

Alexander's son, Peter, was only eleven years old at the time of the assassination, and a regency headed by Alexander's cousin, Prince Paul, took power. Like Alexander, Paul failed to bring about a reconciliation between the Serbs and the other nationalities of Yugoslavia. The royalist government continued its course as a dictatorship holding power through force.

Tito accurately foresaw the development of events, and laid the groundwork for a broad patriotic resistance to the impending Axis invasion. In April, 1941, Germany, Italy, Hungary, and Bulgaria invaded Yugoslavia. The royalist government capitulated within two weeks. The nation was partitioned; Serbia and Croatia became puppet states, and various parts of Yugoslavia were annexed outright by the Axis conquerors. As Tito anticipated, only his Partisan movement was prepared to rally all the nationalities of Yugoslavia against the German, Italian, Hungarian, and Bulgarian invaders and also against rival local groups, including the royalist Serbian forces, the Chetniks, led by Draža Mihailović, and the two openly collaborationist forces, the Croatian Fascist movement, the Ustashi, led by Ante Pavelić, and the Serbian collaborationist forces led by General Milan Nedić.

Tito proved to be an outstanding military strategist, and the Partisans fought heroically against great odds. Without adequate food, clothing, or arms, living under harsh, primitive conditions, they were always outnumbered by the Axis troops that savagely repressed Yugoslavia. Tito personally took direct part in military engagements, and was wounded in action.

It was Tito's Partisans who liberated their nation. The Soviet Red Army that occupied the other countries of Eastern Europe entered Yugoslavia only under terms dictated by Tito, and was required to depart upon the cessation of hostilities.

The close of World War II found Yugoslavia a devastated land. More than 10 percent of the entire population had been killed during the war. The economy was at a standstill. And there were the major problems involved in reuniting a partitioned nation and overcoming the opposition of those groups hostile to Communism. Tito and his followers moved to consolidate their power; the Chetniks and Ustashi were disbanded, Mihailović was tried for treason and executed, and a struggle with the hierarchy of the Roman Catholic Church was climaxed by the trial and imprisonment of Archbishop Stepinac.

Superficially, Yugoslavia seemed much like the Russian-dominated nations of Eastern Europe. This impression was strengthened by Yugoslavia's general support of Soviet foreign policy. Actually, the Yugoslav-Soviet accord was more apparent than real. Despite Yugoslavia's quiet but serious differences with the Soviet Union, however, Tito was generally sympathetic with the Soviet view that the formation of NATO had unnecessarily polarized East-West relations. Moreover, Tito felt that not only Marxist ideology but also historic and ethnic ties between Yugoslavia and Russia would facilitate a special working relationship between the two nations.

But Stalin soon made very clear that he had no intention of respecting the independent wishes of Yugoslavia. Tito steadfastly refused to follow the dictates of Moscow; consequently, Yugoslavia was publicly expelled from the world Communist movement in June, 1948.

Freed from constraint from Moscow, and the beneficiary of American economic aid, the Tito government moved openly to implement major reforms in every sphere of Yugoslav life. Worldwide attention was attracted to certain of these innovations, particularly the decentralization of the economy and the introduction of workers' councils.

One of the major goals of Marxist ideology is, of course, that the means of production be controlled by the workers who actually produce the goods. Until the Yugoslav workers' councils, the Soviet Union, the People's Republic of China, and every other nation espousing a Marxist form of government had a standard form of "state capitalism," in which the government itself operated each economic enterprise, ostensibly on behalf of the workers. Each of these state enterprises was a monopoly in its respective field.

The Yugoslav workers' councils policy, enacted into law by the Yugoslav Parliament in July, 1950, completely reversed this traditional approach. The economy was deliberately decentralized, with the government withdrawing from responsibility for direction and operation of economic enterprises. Full authority for factories and other economic units was shifted directly to the workers in those enterprises, with the actual day-by-day operation supervised by elected councils of workers. Enterprises in the same field were allowed to compete with one another for domestic and international business, and workers in successful enterprises were rewarded with special incentives and benefits.

Decentralization and democratization also were applied in the political sphere. Increasing autonomy was given to the republics and ethnic minorities. Governmental and Communist Party functions were separated, with the party itself being transformed into a new type of organization, the League of Communists of Yugoslavia. Censorship was greatly curtailed. Elections were held in which independent candidates were allowed to challenge and defeat the official candidates for public office.

These unprecedented innovations attracted international attention, excited progressive thinkers and activists throughout the world, and shook the Moscow-led Communist movement to its foundation. Tito contended that Yugoslavia had taken major and unparalleled steps actually to apply immediately in daily life the classic Marxist ideal of giving economic power to the workers, and to implement immediately the classic Marxist goal of the withering away of the state.

In foreign policy, too, Yugoslavia embarked upon an openly independent course, concluding a defensive alliance with Greece and Turkey. And, in a bold attempt to move the world away from the tense and potentially explosive East-West polarization, Tito reached beyond Europe to build new ties with neutralist nations abroad, including India, Indonesia, Burma, and Egypt.

Tito, then, has become triply subversive to the Russian-led Communist movement: He has successfully asserted the right of national self-determination against domination by the Soviet Union; he has pioneered in strengthening a neutralist stance among the "Third World" nations; and he has originated a dangerously imaginative ideological heresy, a variety of Marxism that, by its very nature, serves to undermine monolithic, authoritarian Communism.

Until Stalin's death, the Soviet Union maintained unremitting hostility toward Yugoslavia. The Stalinist opposition went far beyond polemics; in addition to external political and economic pressure constantly exerted upon the Tito government, there were recurring attempts to incite anti-Tito opposition and uprisings within Yugoslavia.

With the advent of Nikita S. Khrushchev to power in the Soviet Union, however, the Russian opposition to Tito softened. In May, 1955, Khrushchev, in his capacity as First Secretary of the Communist Party of the Soviet Union, traveled to Belgrade accompanied by Nikolai Bulganin, Chairman of the Council of Ministers of the Soviet Union. Khrushchev and Bulganin asserted that the Stalinist policy toward Yugoslavia had been in error, and signed a formal agreement with Tito specifically upholding Yugoslavia's right to independent Socialism.

Although Tito welcomed the rapprochement with the Soviet Union, he declined to be drawn into the Russian bloc. And Yugoslavia soon became the target of vitriolic denunciation by Red China. Khrushchev initially agreed with the Chinese; ironicaliy, he himself soon became the chief villain of Chinese ideological propaganda. The Soviet invasion of Hungary in 1956, and the arrest and subsequent execution by the Russians of Hungarian Premier Imre Nagy, who had taken refuge in the Yugoslav Embassy in Budapest, further strained Yugoslav-Russian relations.

Within Yugoslavia, the distinctive Titoist political, social, and economic innovations proceeded apace. Considerable Western attention was attracted to the controversy surrounding Milovan Djilas, formerly one of the three Vice-Presidents of Yugoslavia, who had strongly criticized the Tito government for not proceeding even more rapidly with sweeping liberalization. But the Western press has given comparatively little coverage to the subsequent case of another Vice-President of

Yugoslavia, Aleksandar Ranković, whose viewpoint was just the opposite of that of Djilas. Ranković was a conservative opponent of the Titoist innovations, and was found to have developed a secret police network that dared to spy even upon Tito himself. Although both Djilas and Ranković were removed from public office, each is now at liberty, with complete personal freedom—a tolerance of political dissenters inconceivable in any other Communist nation.

Internationally, Yugoslavia's role in the uncommitted "Third World" continued to grow. In September, 1961, Tito was host in Belgrade to a prestigious conference of heads of state of nonaligned nations, attended by such leaders as Prime Minister Jawaharlal Nehru of India, President Sukarno of Indonesia, President Nkrumah of Ghana, President Nasser of the United Arab Republic, Prime Minister U Nu of Burma, Emperor Haile Selassie of Ethiopia, President Bourguiba of Tunisia, King Hassan II of Morocco, King Mahendra of Nepal, the Presidents of Ceylon, Cuba, Cyprus, Mali, and Somalia, the Prime Ministers of Afghanistan, the Congo, and the Sudan, and other international figures. In all, twenty-six nations were represented by official delegations, and three additional nations sent official observers.

The sudden overthrow of Khrushchev as leader of the Soviet Union in October, 1964, revealed dangerous instability in Moscow. The subsequent renunciation of Khrushchev's "de-Stalinization" policies by the new heads of the Soviet state, Party Secretary Leonid I. Brezhnev and Premier Aleksei N. Kosygin, seemed an ominous portent of more rigid Russian views upholding orthodox Soviet Communism. This portent became tragic reality in August, 1968, when Russian, Polish, East German, Hungarian, and Bulgarian troops invaded and occupied the Czechoslovak Socialist Republic.

Following the occupation of Czechoslovakia in 1968, the Soviet Union hastily proclaimed a new doctrine of "Socialist commonwealth," arrogating to Russia the right to intervene unilaterally in the domestic affairs of any Communist nation. This new Soviet policy is the antithesis of independent, national Communism developing naturally and distinctively, as espoused by Tito; and it poses a direct threat to the very independence of Yugoslavia as a nation.

The twenty-fifth anniversary of this unique state found Yugoslavia true to herself, having courageously and tenaciously followed a consistent policy of domestic innovation and international neutrality based upon principle. As the power politics of East and West have been shaped and dominated by the exercise of naked power, and the Soviet Union has been convulsed by its attempt to preserve and perpetuate a rigid, obsolete, authoritarian, monolithic structure, the Socialist Federal Republic of Yugoslavia, a small nation with limited resources, has proven what independent national Communism can be in terms both of domestic social uplift and of genuine co-existence promoting world peace.

Tito continues as unchallenged leader of the state he founded. General Secretary of the Communist Party of Yugoslavia since 1937, he became General Secretary of its successor organization, the League of Communists of Yugoslavia, upon formation of the LCY in 1952. Elected Marshal of Yugoslavia by the historic Second Session of the Anti-Fascist Council of People's Liberation of Yugoslavia in 1943, he also became Prime Minister of the new government of Yugoslavia in 1945. In 1953, he relinquished the post of Prime Minister to become President of the Federal Republic.

In addition to his public responsibilities, Tito has a family life. He is the father of two sons, one from each of his two previous marriages, and is also a grandfather. He and the present Mrs. Broz, the former Jovanka Budisavljević, were married in 1952.

Each document presented in this volume is of prime historical significance. The first selection defines the character of the
Partisan resistance movement, and is followed immediately by
the first political document of New Yugoslavia, Tito's address
to the First Session of the Anti-Fascist Council of People's
Liberation in 1942. This in turn is followed by his address in
1943 to the historic Second Session of the Anti-Fascist Council which became the provisional government of Yugoslavia.
By the time of Tito's address to the Third Session of the
Anti-Fascist Council in 1945, Yugoslavia had triumphed over
her Axis occupiers. Taken together, these four documents provide a unique, authoritative insight into the development of
Partisan victory.

Then, in his report to the Fifth Congress of the Communist
Party of Yugoslavia in 1948, Tito not only reviews the establishment of New Yugoslavia, by now expelled from the world
Communist movement, but also rebuts in detail the accusations of Moscow. In the subsequent selection Tito analyzes the
most widely discussed innovation of New Yugoslavia, the
workers' councils system of economic management.

The next two documents, Tito's 1960 address to the United
Nations and his subsequent address to the Belgrade Conference of Nonaligned Countries, are internationally significant
statements concerning foreign affairs. In the first, he summa-
rizes the principles and objectives of Yugoslavia's foreign policy, and in the second he is spokesman for the goals and aspirations of the developing nations of the "Third World."

In the final two selections, Tito sums up. In his address on
Current International and Domestic Issues, he strongly re-
bukes the Soviet Union for the invasion and occupation of the
Czechoslovak Socialist Republic by the Warsaw Pact nations in
1968. As in his 1948 anti-Stalin address twenty years before,
Tito again contrasts the Yugoslav and Russian systems of

Communism. And, in his historic address at the Jubilee Session of the Anti-Fascist Council in 1968, he reviews in detail the first quarter-century of New Yugoslavia, expounding the distinctive history and unique character of the Socialist Federal Republic of Yugoslavia.

One note of caution, however. This book does not presume to be a definitive work on Josip Broz Tito as a person, or on the Socialist Federal Republic of Yugoslavia as a historical and political entity or a social and economic system. The complete works of Tito alone would constitute many volumes of this size. Rather, this book is intended to be an introduction to the subject, presenting key authoritative material by Tito previously unavailable outside Yugoslavia. It is the earnest hope of the editor that this work will serve to advance the general understanding of, and stimulate interest in, that remarkable combination, Tito the man and Yugoslavia the nation.

Henry M. Christman
Belgrade and New York

THE ESSENTIAL TITO

I

The Tasks Before the People's Liberation Partisan Detachments

Bulletin No. 1 of the GHQ, People's Liberation Detachments of Yugoslavia

August 10, 1941

The Partisan resistance movement was a unique development in Yugoslavia. Unlike other modern Yugoslav political movements, which were clearly dominated by one or another of the nation's ethnic groups and directed toward the special interests of that group, the Partisan movement was from the very first a multi-ethnic movement. The patriotic heroism of the Partisans and their honorable treatment of noncombatants attracted respect and support throughout Yugoslavia, even from Yugoslavs strongly opposed to Communism.

Following herewith is the complete text of the official charter of the Partisan resistance movement, written by Tito.

I
Tasks Before the Partisans

First. The People's Liberation Partisan Detachments in all areas of Yugoslavia (in Serbia, Croatia, Slovenia, Montenegro, Bosnia and Herzegovina, Macedonia, the Vojvodina, the Sandžak and Dalmatia) have as their main aim: the liberation of the peoples of Yugoslavia from the invader, and the fight against the invader's local agents who are assisting in the work of oppression and terrorization of our peoples.

Second. The greatest enemy of the freedom and independence of our people is German Fascism, then all its other Fascist hangers-on who are engaged in marauding up and down the country. Consequently, it is the bounden duty of all patriots to fight mercilessly until these Fascist bands are destroyed to the last man.

Third. The Partisan detachments are called People's Liber-

3

ation detachments because they are not fighting units of any particular political party or group—nor in this particular case of the Communist Party, regardless of the fact that Communists are fighting in the front rank; rather they are fighting units of the peoples of Yugoslavia, which ought to be joined by all patriots capable of armed struggle against the invader, regardless of their political convictions.

Fourth. In the common struggle against the enemy of our people the Partisan detachments have numerous tasks. They must destroy all objects of use to the Fascist invaders: railways, bridges, factories, workshops, munition and arms dumps. They must use all their powers to prevent the enemy from confiscating grain, cattle, and other food supplies from the peasants. Requisitioned grain, cattle, and other food supplies must be taken away from the enemy by force and distributed among the people, the necessary amount being kept to supply the detachments. The Partisan detachments must prevent the collection of taxes and other dues, for at the present moment all these things help the enemy to carry on his war of conquest and to continue the subjugation of our people.

Fifth. The Partisan detachments must defend, by force of arms, settlements, towns, and villages, from Fascist outrages. They must protect the people's property from enemy looting.

Sixth. The Partisan detachments must destroy Fascist units whenever they come across them, especially the officers, Gestapo men, and Blackshirts, etc. They must also be merciless in destroying their local henchmen, the various domestic traitors and *agents provocateurs* who are handing over, in great numbers, the best sons of the people to the Fascist butchers, licking the boots of the occupier like fawning dogs and terrorizing our people.

Seventh. The Partisan detachments must be tireless in stimulating the resistance of the people, raising insurrections among the people and putting themselves in charge as the militant hard core. What has happened in Partisan warfare so far has shown that the question of a widespread national uprising has been neglected; so it is essential to make good this shortcoming, otherwise the Partisans may be cut off from the masses who are ready to fight for their just cause.

Eighth. The political line of the Partisan detachments must be: the People's Liberation Anti-Fascist Front of all the nationalities of Yugoslavia, regardless of their political and religious beliefs.

Ninth. There should be no exclusiveness in forming Partisan detachments; the opportunity for wide initiative in forming Partisan detachments should be given. Once they have been formed, Partisan detachments should be immediately linked with district and regional HQs and put under their command.

Tenth. HQs and junior commanders of Partisan detachments must take every precaution to prevent the enemy from infiltrating spies and *agents provocateurs* into the Partisan ranks. If they should appear, they must be shot immediately and their names published.

Eleventh. HQs and junior commanders of Partisan detachments must pay special attention to discipline in the detachments. Looting, treason or any other breach of discipline, must in every case be severely punished.

Twelfth. HQs must be responsible for the food supplies of their fighting men, and for equipping them, etc. Food supplies should be organized in consultation with the committees of the People's Liberation Front, which has the task of collecting for the People's Liberation fund. In cases where there are no such committees yet, it is necessary, with the voluntary consent of the peasants and citizens, to insure food supplies or to buy provisions with cash.

Thirteenth. All Partisan detachments and their HQs, from Croatia, Serbia, Slovenia, Montenegro, Bosnia and Herzegovina, Vojvodina, Dalmatia, Macedonia, and the Sandžak, come under the Supreme Command of the GHQ of the People's Liberation detachments of Yugoslavia.

With a view to battle co-ordination and successful operational procedure, HQs must be well linked up, one with another.

Fourteenth. HQs and junior commanders must be responsible for the necessary hospital equipment and personnel for the sick and wounded.

Fifteenth. With the development of a widespread uprising of the people's masses the necessary commands will be set up; and so it is essential that the HQs and junior commanders of Partisan detachments be on the lookout for tried and trusted commanders and commissars to take over the leadership of the insurgent masses.

Sixteenth. Whenever strategic and other circumstances are favorable a number of Partisan detachments may, where needed, be merged into larger military formations in order to facilitate the conduct of major operations.

II

Address at the First Session, Anti-Fascist Council of People's Liberation (AVNOJ)

Bihać, Yugoslavia
November 26, 1942

In 1942, the Partisan movement in Yugoslavia faced stagger-
ing odds. Not only Yugoslavia, but all Allied territory of con-
tinental Europe except Russia had been occupied by the Axis
conquerors. The Soviet Union, Britain, and the British-held
area of North Africa were under heavy Axis attack. The
poorly armed, poorly fed Partisans were outnumbered, and
completely isolated in the mountains of Yugoslavia, cut off
from Allied assistance by land, sea, or air.

Despite these circumstances, however, Tito not only contin-
ued effective military resistance, but also proceeded to de-
velop the political side of the Partisan movement. Following
herewith is the complete text of his address to the First Session
of the Anti-Fascist Council of People's Liberation, the first
political document of New Yugoslavia.

II
First Session of AVNOJ

Comrades, brothers and sisters, delegates of the Anti-Fascist Council of People's Liberation of Yugoslavia: I welcome you on behalf of Supreme Headquarters, on behalf of the fighting men, commanders and political commissars of our heroic People's Liberation Army and Partisan detachments of Yugoslavia.

I consider it a great honor that the opportunity has offered itself for me to welcome you here today at this historic assembly, after the great and tough and bloody struggle which our people have had to wage during the past eighteen months.

I open this historic assembly of the Anti-Fascist Council of People's Liberation of Yugoslavia, and I should now like to say a few words to you.

The result of the long, tough, and bloody struggle—an un-

equal struggle, because we went into battle almost barehanded
—the result of this struggle is that today we have the opportunity to meet here, to create an instrument, a body which together with the Supreme Headquarters of the People's Liberation Army and Partisan detachments of Yugoslavia, and together with the People's Liberation committees, will be the
backbone of our struggle; it will organize the home front, it
will organize our devastated country economically and
politically—in so far as such a thing can be done in these
circumstances—in order that we may bring this bitter struggle
to a victorious conclusion.

Comrades, we have no possibility of setting up a legal
government, because international relations and conditions do
not permit it as yet. But, comrades, we have a right to one
thing—namely: we have the right in these critical circumstances to set up a political body, a political instrument, to
rally the people's masses, to rally our people and conduct
them, together with our heroic army, into the new battles
ahead of us, battles that will be exceedingly bitter. We have no
authorities in our territory with the exception of our People's
Liberation committees which have been set up by the people
themselves. We do not recognize the various Fascist puppet
governments, and that is precisely why, here in this land, in
our own land, soaked with the blood of the best sons of our
people, we have to create conditions in which our people can
—in such circumstances as the present—contribute their utmost to the People's Liberation struggle. While we were a small
Partisan army and had only small Partisan detachments, the
requirements were not so great. Today those small Partisan
detachments have become a mighty People's Liberation Army
which is not merely the equal of, but is superior to, the enemy
in stamina and morale, in spite of the enemy's technical superiority. And so it is that the requirements are very much
greater than before when every village, district, or community

was able to feed its own fighting men. It is necessary to organize the authority, the political power, which will be able to mobilize, to make use of all the latent power possessed by our people and to channel it in one general direction—into the battle against the criminal Fascist invaders, and against their allies, the traitors in our midst—the Ustashi, the Chetniks, and others.

I am happy to see here today the best sons of our people, patriots, true representatives of our people who have been steeled in this bitter and bloody struggle. They are no longer, as was once the case, representatives selected by canvassers; they are men who have grown in this superhuman struggle out of the very heart of the people, men who have gone into battle prepared to lay down their lives. I am happy to see here today what is really the flower of our nation.

Comrades, a heavy burden, a great responsibility, falls upon our Anti-Fascist Council of People's Liberation of Yugoslavia. We possess, so to speak, nothing. We have only the weapons which we captured with the blood of our best fighting men. Our country is devastated; our people are enduring terrible sufferings and misery, hungry, naked, barefooted, exposed to the bestial terror of the Chetniks, the Ustashi, and the invader. But we have one thing—the unswerving firmness and faith of our afflicted people that victory will be theirs. Our morale is high, not only the morale of our army—which has astonished the whole world—but also the morale of the people. Just look at the burnt-down villages. Nearby, in the freezing cold, in shacks or under the open sky, in the woods beside a fire, you can see peasants and their wives; but they do not bewail their fate—they say: "Dear brothers, fight! We are prepared to give our last crust if it will help you to defeat our common enemy." That is the kind of morale that is rarely seen, something that the Yugoslav peoples can be proud of.

It is only natural that the organism which we are creating

here, which has grown up from below, should bear a heavy responsibility and have a huge task to fulfill. Our army needs clothing—and we have no factories. Our army needs footwear—and we have no boot factories. Our army needs weapons—and we have no arms factories. And our army needs food. All these things fall upon this great forum which our people have created as the nucleus of their authority. I think there is no one among you who is afraid of these hard tasks and great responsibilities. I think you are all prepared to sacrifice everything in the coming struggle which promises victory to our arms. We have done battle and will continue to do battle with the enemy in spite of his superiority in arms. Hand in hand with you, comrades, who are the representatives of our peoples, our Supreme Headquarters will easily be able to surmount all the difficulties that lie ahead. Today we accept these difficulties, and overcome them, more easily than six months ago. Today the prospect is clear—it's as clear as the sun that victory is on the side of the Allies. The Hitlerite and other Fascist bands are today suffering defeat after defeat. The heroic Red Army has been delivering deadly blows to the German Fascist hordes and to Hitler's satellites. Stalingrad, the fortress of the whole of progressive humanity, has been defended. Hundreds of thousands of German soldiers have perished in this and earlier offensives, beneath the walls of this city-of-flint. The Hitlerite Fascists hurl themselves in every direction, like wild beasts in a cage; but there is no hope for them. In their death throes they will perhaps try to wreak their rage upon the weaker, occupied countries, upon the occupied nations, but we can tell them that in Yugoslavia they will have a really tough time. Today we have an army; today we have arms, everything from rifles to field guns. We can measure up to them all right. You may rest assured that their power in our country is not sufficient to realize and put into practice their diabolical intentions, that is to destroy us. We have never lost faith, and today least of all do we doubt that victory is ours. Consequently, at this moment, when the hearts of all subjugated peoples are beating with joy as they see the inevitable defeat of the Fascist beasts, we go forward, boldly and full of hope and faith, to meet all the difficulties awaiting us, convinced that by working together and fighting together we shall carry our long struggle and our sufferings to a triumphant close.

Finally, I should like to emphasize that all that we have achieved so far in our struggle is in some measure due to our great Slav brothers the Russians and all the peoples of the Soviet Union. A deep faith in the strength and might of the Soviet Union, in the strength and might of the Red Army, was the sustenance that supported us while we were surmounting all the difficulties that we have had to face in the past eighteen months.

I wish you, the great national forum, the Anti-Fascist Council of People's Liberation of Yugoslavia, every success in your future work for the welfare of our peoples, for the welfare of our valiant People's Liberation Army, and in the interests of the unity of all the nationalities in Yugoslavia, for that is the foundation which is now being built, the foundation of brotherhood, unity, and concord, which no one will ever be able to destroy. This historic assembly is proof of the unity of our peoples, Serbs, Croats, Slovenes, Montenegrins, Moslems, and others, regardless of their faith and nationality; and it is, at the same time, a guarantee that progress is being made in creating a better and happier future for our people.

> Long live our great Ally the Soviet Union!
> Long live the heroic Red Army!
> Long live our Allies—Britain and America!
> Death to Fascism— Freedom to the people!

III

Address at the Second Session, Anti-Fascist Council of People's Liberation (AVNOJ)

Jajce, Yugoslavia
November 29, 1943

By late 1943, the tide of war had shifted, its new direction dramatically highlighted by the collapse of Fascist Italy, a prime objective of Tito's military and political strategy.

The historic Second Session of the Anti-Fascist Council of People's Liberation marked the official foundation and beginning of the Socialist Federal Republic of Yugoslavia. Following herewith is the complete text of Marshal Tito's address on that major occasion.

III
Second Session of AVNOJ

I

Our People's Liberation struggle can be divided into four stages. These are as follows:

First. The capitulation of Yugoslavia and the beginning of the people's uprising, which from its outset featured the formation of numerous Partisan detachments for fighting against the occupier;

Second. The growth of the Partisan detachments into regular military units, battalions, brigades, and divisions, and the creation of the People's Liberation Army of Yugoslavia;

Third. The growth of the People's Liberation committees into a real people's authority, and the setting up of the Anti-Fascist Council of People's Liberation of Yugoslavia;

Fourth. The stage at which we are now, and that is—the

15

transformation of the Anti-Fascist Council of People's Liberation of Yugoslavia from a general political body into the highest legislative body, and the setting up of the National Committee of Liberation of Yugoslavia as a provisional national
government.

The first stage. The causes of such a quick capitulation of
Yugoslavia and the enslavement of our country by German,
Italian, Hungarian, and Bulgarian invaders are today quite
clear to the majority of our people. The twenty-year-old oppression of the various nationalities of Yugoslavia (such as the
Croats, the Macedonians, the Slovenes and others) by a handful of Great-Serb hegemonists; further, the unprecedented corruption of the ruling circles inside the country and their affili-
ations with the most reactionary circles abroad, especially in
Germany and Italy, for the purpose of keeping themselves in
power; then the unprecedented treachery and espionage inside
the Yugoslav Army, especially in the General Staff—all
these things were causes of the catastrophic and disgraceful
defeat of the Yugoslav armies in the war. This defeat had catastrophic consequences for the people of Yugoslavia. The
king and government fled abroad with the group of people responsible for such a fate having overtaken the country. Yugoslavia was carved up and became the booty of aggressors such
as history has rarely seen. In the country there broke out unprecedented terror, and exterminations were carried out not
only of the most progressive elements but of the entire Serbian
population of Croatia, Bosnia and Herzegovina, and Vojvodina, and of the Slovene population of Slovenia, and so on.
The German and Italian aggressors brought to power in Croatia the bloody Ustashi monsters, and in Serbia the loathsome
traitor Nedić; and with the help of these men they began to
execute their diabolical plan for the extermination of Slavs in
the Balkans. In this grievous situation, I can say with certitude
the most grievous situation in the history of our peoples, there

was one single organization in the country, one which for twenty years had, so to speak, been outside the law and had been persecuted by all who came to power in Yugoslavia— and now it has placed in the service of its enslaved country all its experience and organizational skill, and all its tried and trusted fighters. It was only the Communist Party which led the people into armed revolt, which never lost heart but raised high the standard of the Liberation struggle, and which, together with its people, has remained steadfast.

The formation of Partisan detachments began first of all in Serbia, Bosnia and Herzegovina, then the general people's uprising in Montenegro in July, then the extension of the Partisan movement to Croatia and Slovenia, etc. All this showed that our country, although enslaved, remained unconquered and that our people were prepared to make the greatest sacrifices for their liberation. The small, almost unarmed, Partisan detachments began to grow quickly and developed into large units which seized weapons from the enemy, inflicted increasingly heavy blows upon the enemy, and showed that they could not be destroyed in spite of all the German, Italian, Bulgarian, and Hungarian occupying forces which were sent into battle for the purpose of stamping out the Partisan movement in various parts of the country.

Withstanding in this way all enemy onslaughts and growing with increasing frequency into large Partisan units, the Partisan detachments were formed into regular military units, by a decree of the Supreme Command in the autumn of 1942; that is to say, the People's Liberation Army of Yugoslavia came into being.

The second stage of the People's Liberation struggle began. Brigades, divisions, and army corps were formed, and whole areas were liberated from the enemy and their Ustashi and Chetnik henchmen. Our young People's Liberation Army showed at its very outset that it was capable of discharging even the most onerous tasks. Numerous towns were liberated, for example: Livno, Glamoč, Mrkonjićgrad, Jajce, Ključ, Bihać, Krupa, Slunj, etc. The creation of the People's Liberation Army gave a new impetus to the uprising in areas which had been relatively quiet until then.

In this period the People's Liberation struggle assumed an increasingly stable character and because of that gained the confidence of an ever increasing number of people in all parts of Yugoslavia.

The People's Liberation committees, which until that time had been set up in liberated territory, now began to be set up in semi-liberated territory as well, and even in occupied territory, for this new nucleus of people's authority was becoming increasingly popular among the people and in increasing measure gained their confidence. While at the beginning the People's Liberation committees had been set up more as auxiliary bodies of the Partisan detachments for the conduct of the Liberation War, by the time the People's Liberation Army was created these committees had been transformed into the sole real people's authority. In addition to assisting Partisan units and the People's Liberation Army, they now had many other tasks placed in front of them. The third stage began, in which it was imperative that a single general-political national body be set up, one which should be a central organ and which should unite all of them and set up new People's Liberation committees.

The historic assembly of the Anti-Fascist Council of People's Liberation of Yugoslavia was convoked in Bihać. At that session great and important resolutions were passed. For the first time since the occupation of the country a central political body composed of representatives of all the nationalities of Yugoslavia was set up. For the first time there had been sessions of a national representative body which had sprung up from the people, had sprung up in the most grievous hour in their history, a body before which the Supreme Headquarters was answerable for its performance to date.

The setting up of the Anti-Fascist Council of People's Liberation of Yugoslavia was one of the greatest achievements of the People's Liberation struggle up to that time. The foundations were laid on which could be built a new, more just social order in the territories of Yugoslavia; the foundations were laid on which could be built true brotherhood and the equality of all the nationalities of Yugoslavia, the foundations of a just, truly democratic people's government. With the setting up of the Provincial Anti-Fascist Council of People's Liberation of Croatia, and before that the Slovene Liberation Front and its executive body, the principles of equality for all the nationalities of Yugoslavia began to be put into practice, and the age-old aspirations of the individual nationalities of Yugoslavia to govern themselves began to be realized.

In the course of the year following the setting up of the Anti-Fascist Council of People's Liberation of Yugoslavia great changes have taken place, not only in Yugoslavia but in the whole world. We have had, especially in the past year, to fight bitter and bloody battles with the occupier. Great but glorious tasks were placed before the People's Liberation Army. In the six-month period from January right up until June, 1943, we withstood two large-scale enemy offensives, the fourth and the fifth, which were launched with a view to destroying the People's Liberation Army and reoccupying our liberated territory. These were heavy ordeals for our People's Liberation Army. We bore the brunt of tremendous strains, and here the sons of our nation showed an unprecedented heroism and self-sacrifice such as will be the pride of future generations of our people. In spite of the enemy's enormous numerical and technical superiority, they were unable to destroy the nucleus of our People's Liberation Army. On the contrary they suffered enormous losses, and we by our bitter and bloody struggle gained the sympathy and admiration of the whole world—that is one point, and another is that the Allies began to recognize our People's Liberation Army in that they sent a military mission to the Supreme Command of the People's Liberation Army and Partisan detachments of Yugoslavia. In the course of these great battles, especially during the fifth offensive, we suffered heavy losses. Thousands of the best sons of the people were killed. Among the fallen were Nurija Pozderac, Veselin Masleša, Sima Milošević, all of them members of the executive committee of the Anti-Fascist Council of People's Liberation of Yugoslavia, as well as several members of the Council. These are heavy and irreplaceable losses. Let us honor these glorious sons of our people who gave their precious lives for a better and happier future for the people of Yugoslavia.

Oceans of precious blood from our people had to be shed, tens of thousands of the best sons of our people had to lay down their lives in the course of this two-year unequal struggle with the enemy, before the truth about the real state of affairs in Yugoslavia finally blazed through to the world outside. Never before, perhaps, has a small nation paid so dearly for persuading the world that the blood shed in Yugoslavia was its own blood, not the blood of the shameful traitors whose leaders are now enjoying the hospitality of Allied countries.

An unprecedented deception imposed upon all honest men in the world outside has been unmasked during the past year. For two whole years and more the treacherous London government deceived the whole world by talking about the struggle being waged in Yugoslavia by its minister, Draža Mihailović. That the irony might be the greater, the Chetnik bands with the minister-traitor at their head were engaged in battle all that time—and still are!—on the side of the occupier against the People's Liberation Army and Partisan detachments. But nothing stopped these monsters from passing off the victories of the People's Liberation Army as their own. During the fourth offensive the traitor Draža Mihailović came to an agreement with the Germans, Italians and Ustashi to collaborate with them in dealing a death-blow to our People's Liberation Army. Numerous documents, which fell into our hands during our offensive against the Chetniks of Draža Mihailović, clearly expose the diabolical plan and unprecedented treachery of these fiends. As is already known to our public, during our great and glorious battles on the river Neretva and at Gornji Vakuf, Draža Mihailović had conscripted some eighteen thousand men in Serbia, the Sandžak, Montenegro, Herzegovina, and Eastern Bosnia, and he transported them to the Neretva to stab us in the back. To the crowning glory of the First, Second, Third, and Seventh divisions and units of the Ninth Dalmatian Division, not only were the Germans, Italians, and Ustashi smashed in the battle on the Neretva, but our troops passed over to a decisive offensive against the Chetniks of Draža Mihailović and drove them from the Neretva to Kolašin, where they delivered a knock-out blow and liquidated the Chetniks as a serious military force.

These are all facts which the traitor government-in-exile has been unable to conceal from the world. Their deception has finally been exposed.

As a result of events outside our country, that is, as a result of the victories of the glorious Red Army on the Eastern Front and the annihilation of Hitler's élite armies, conditions were created for the victories of the other Allies, the British and Americans in Africa, conditions were created for the Allied landings in Sicily, and finally in Italy, and for the capitulation of Hitler's chief partner, Fascist Italy. Here I must emphasize that a great part was played in the elimination of Italy from the conflict by our People's Liberation Army which throughout the whole war pinned down sixteen to twenty Italian divisions. Just before the capitulation of Italy, units of our People's Liberation Army, going over again to the offensive after the fifth enemy offensive, liberated almost the whole of Eastern Bosnia, the greater part of Central Bosnia and the Bosnian Krajina.

With the capitulation of Italy and the disarming of thirteen Italian divisions in Yugoslavia, our People's Liberation Army not only acquired a great amount of military equipment but it also increased its ranks by at least eighty thousand fighting men and liberated large areas in Dalmatia and Slovenia and elsewhere. Consequently conditions were created for new victorious operations by units of the People's Liberation Army on the one hand, while on the other hand our People's Liberation Army had gained the reputation among the Allies of being a serious military factor, for today not only do the Allies count on it as their ally but the Fascist occupiers realize that it is an adversary which is tying down a large number of divisions. Following upon the capitulation of Italy an unparalleled impetus was given to the people's uprising in Slovenia, Dalmatia, and indeed in the rest of Croatia. Thus there is today no region of Yugoslavia left untouched by the flame of national uprising. By the first of November this year enormous areas of the country had been liberated. A large part of Dalmatia was liberated, a large part of the Croatian Littoral, a large part of Slovenia, the Bosnian Krajina, the whole of Eastern Bosnia, a large part of Central Bosnia, the whole of the Sandžak, a large part of Montenegro, and a part of Herzegovina.

Some of our divisions have already passed the border between the Sandžak and Serbia. Once again the liberation of the Serbian people from the German and Bulgarian invaders, Nedić's troops, and the Chetnik bands of Draža Mihailović, has begun. One of the significant facts is that our Partisan forces in Macedonia have recently achieved considerable success and have for the second time taken Kičevo and Debar, thus creating conditions for a stronger growth of the Partisan movement in Macedonia. The Partisan movement in Macedonia is closely linked with the Partisan movement in Albania and Greece and at the same time it has become an important contributory factor to the development of the Partisan movement even in Bulgaria.

One of the most successful achievements of our people's uprising, one of great historic significance, was the liberation of Istria and the Slovene Littoral, after the capitulation of Italy. In spite of the persistence of the Fascists, twenty years of slavery failed to deprive our enslaved brothers, the Slovene and Croatian people, of their national character or to weaken their yearning for unity with their own brothers and the other peoples of Yugoslavia.

As has been shown earlier, the situation in Yugoslavia and in the world has completely changed in the past year. Thanks to the victories of the Red Army, Hitler's war machine is on the brink of catastrophe; a victory over this, the greatest enemy of mankind is not far off. In the course of this year the Fascist bloc has disintegrated. Italy has been eliminated from the conflict. Even greater confusion and disintegration reign among Hitler's satellites. The relations between the Allies, the Soviet Union, Britain, and America, are becoming increasingly close; and this was very much in evidence at the Moscow conference of representatives of the three great Allied powers. All these factors also have an enormous significance for our People's Liberation struggle. Faith in imminent victory and in final liberation for our people from the yoke of the occupier is gaining ground among increasingly widespread sections of the population; and this can be seen in the large numbers of new recruits who are flocking wholesale to the ranks of the People's Liberation Army and in the fact that many outstanding political, cultural, and other public figures from all parts of

Yugoslavia are joining our People's Liberation struggle. From
another point of view, all these things bring influence to bear
upon the increasingly swift disintegration of the puppet state
machines of Pavelić and Nedić and, consequently, upon the
weakening of the occupier's position in our country.

But one thing has not changed in the course of the past
year, in spite of all the factors which we have just mentioned.
And that is the policy of the traitor-government, which is now
in Cairo and which, unfortunately, is still recognized by our
Allies as the legitimate representative of the Yugoslav peoples.
I have no intention in this short report of going into the details of why this is so, why the Allies tolerate this government
which has no support among the people, since it has been co-
operating through its minister Draža Mihailović with the occupier for two and a half years in fighting against the People's
Liberation Army, in other words, against the Yugoslav peoples.
I have no intention of going into the details of why the Allies
tolerate a government which is blatantly reactionary and
Great-Serb in its orientation, as can be seen from its composition, for it includes such people as the notorious "man-of-Janu-
ary-the-sixth," Pera Živković, and others. But one thing I can
say: there is not a single fighting man in the People's Liberation Army and Partisan detachments who would fail to feel
sick at heart and galled every time he thought about that government, which has so many crimes on its conscience and
which ought to be on the list of war criminals, still sitting and
enjoying the hospitality of our Allies. We are very well aware
that this government is doing all it can to smuggle itself back
at any cost (and that goes for the king, too), before the people
utter their decisive word on their future. We know that certain
reactionary circles abroad are helping the government and
king in their machinations. But we know, also, that the vast
majority of progressive democratic elements in the Allied
countries sincerely desire our people to decide their future for

themselves and to create the kind of state system which they themselves find necessary.

We have been slandered, and we still are being slandered, from all sides—but the pattern is always the same. All the occupiers and quislings—the hireling traitors, the Ustashi, the Nedićites, and the Chetniks of Draža Mihailović in the country and their masters abroad—have said (and still say) that our People's Liberation struggle in Yugoslavia is purely a Communist affair: Bolshevization of the country, an attempt by Communists to seize power, the abolition of private property, the destruction of the church and religion, the destruction of culture, and so on and so forth. These slanders are old and threadbare. They have their origin in Goebbels' kitchen and they have now become a sort of *gleichgeschaltet* fodder for Goebbels' counterparts to feed the population of the "New Europe" with; and they are now trying to export it outside Europe, as well. But very few people believe these lies any longer, least of all the Yugoslav peoples. Our struggle for existence is too bloody and bitter, and so many, too many, of our people have drained the cup of suffering, for someone, making use of these threadbare slanders, to turn them from the path of their great and glorious struggle for independence, for a better and happier future. The times are past when a handful of reactionaries could ascribe (and sometimes with some success) such and similar matters to the Communists of Yugoslavia, in order to isolate them from the people. During the great People's Liberation struggle the peoples of Yugoslavia have become convinced that the Communists are the most faithful sons of their people, always prepared for the greatest sacrifices for the happiness of the people.

Bearing this in mind, and especially bearing in mind the development of the general people's uprising as a whole, the liberation of increasingly large areas of territory and the increasingly large tasks in front of our peoples and the development of events abroad, it is essential to take steps in good time for the further successful development of the People's Liberation struggle; all the necessary measures must be undertaken to insure that our peoples obtain a state system founded on the brotherhood and unity of all the nationalities of Yugoslavia and guaranteeing true liberty and democracy to all sections of the community. The monarchy has completely discredited itself in the eyes of the people during twenty-three years. It was not the protagonist of democratic principles, but of the dictatorship of the most reactionary clique. The monarchy did not provide a link for the brotherhood of the peoples of Yugoslavia and a foundation for the creation of a powerful national state community. The monarchy was the protagonist of Great-Serb hegemony and oppression of other peoples. In 1929 the late King Alexander dissolved Parliament and set up a dictatorship. He introduced a régime of terror and oppression. From the very beginning King Peter II became a focal point for the gathering together of the very reactionaries who had brought ruin upon the country. Furthermore, all this time he has been lending his support to that shameful arch-traitor Draža Mihailović and his voivods. The evidence for this has been proved hundreds and thousands of times and all our peoples know it. In this connection, only a democratic republican form of government can insure that such disasters never again come upon our people.

Such is the situation in the fourth stage of the development of our People's Liberation struggle. Consequently our national representative body is faced with the task of undertaking all the necessary measures and of justifying the confidence which the vast majority of the freedom-loving people of Yugoslavia have placed in it. In this fourth stage, in relation to internal and external events, the need arises to create national bodies, political and legislative, and also the executive bodies arising out of them, which will be able to overcome all difficulties and which will be worthy representatives of the Yugoslav peoples, both inside the country and outside it, and capable of preventing any attempt, from whatever quarter, at frustrating the aspirations for which our peoples have shed so much blood in this great Liberation struggle. Today it is necessary for the Anti-Fascist Council of People's Liberation of Yugoslavia to become in actual fact the highest legislative and executive body of the Yugoslav peoples. The time is now ripe to create an executive body in the form of a provisional government, empowered to carry out all the functions of a proper national government.

Today we have the Anti-Fascist Council of People's Liberation of Yugoslavia, which was set up a year ago. In this Council all the peoples of Yugoslavia are represented, all sections of the community are represented. For the first time in their history our peoples are sending into an assembly of their own representatives from among themselves, whom they elect freely and in whom they have, without any doubt, complete confidence.

Naturally, when a people takes such a momentous step as the setting up of its highest executive body, in this particular case the setting up of the National Committee of Liberation of Yugoslavia, it may, at the beginning, come across certain obstacles and misconceptions, even among our Allies abroad. The more so since there is a certain pseudo-government still in existence abroad. But the Yugoslav peoples in the course of the past two years and nine months of bitter and bloody struggle for their freedom and independence have earned the right to decide their future for themselves, and that right is completely in accord with the Atlantic Charter. We are convinced that our Allies will not misunderstand this historical step that has been taken by our peoples, but that on the contrary they will do all they can to give our people moral and material help and support through the very representative body which the people in the country have themselves elected.

II

And now a few words about our glorious People's Liberation
Army. We boldly assert that the creation of a people's army
under such conditions as those under which ours was created
is unique in history. Out of unarmed Partisan detachments,
with no arms and munitions factories, no arsenals and various
military stockpiles, without help from any quarter, an army of
nearly a quarter of a million has been created—not in peace-
time, but in a period of the most frightful and bloody struggle
which the peoples of Yugoslavia have ever had to wage. This
is an achievement on which the Yugoslav people can pride
themselves, on which future generations will pride themselves.

The creation of our People's Liberation Army, taking place
under such conditions, was an immensely difficult task. We had
no military academies or schools, we had no officer corps. Everything was conceived and born in the course of the struggle
itself. On May 1, 1943, the Supreme Command of the People's Liberation Army and Partisan detachments of Yugoslavia issued a decree introducing officer and NCO ranks into
the People's Liberation Army. Peasants and workers, students
and the rest of our national intelligentsia, who had grown and
developed in the People's Liberation struggle, became officers
in our people's army. These are the flower of the nation,
whom the fighting men themselves have promoted from their
ranks. The people of Yugoslavia can be proud of such officers
and NCOs.

What we are doing here now is also of tremendous significance in our relations with the outside world, in our relations
with our Allies, because in this way our people have shown
clearly and decisively, through their representative body, that
they are exercising their will. But it should be mentioned that
all the officers of the former Yugoslav Army who joined our

ranks from the very beginning have assumed a worthy place in our army. Naturally their numbers would be greater, if such a large number of Yugoslav officers were not in German captivity, thus being denied the possibility of participating in the People's Liberation struggle. Our Supreme Command has promoted officers and created new ones to a total of more than five thousand. I, on behalf of the Supreme Command of the People's Liberation Army and Partisan detachments of Yugoslavia, hereby request this high national forum to ratify the decree of May 1, 1943, and the decree of November 1, 1943, concerning the creation and promotion of officers in the People's Liberation Army of Yugoslavia.

The Supreme Command of the People's Liberation Army and Partisan detachments of Yugoslavia has issued a decree for the introduction of military decorations, as follows: 1. Order of People's Hero. 2. Order of the Partisan Star, first class. 3. Order of the Partisan Star, second class. 4. Order of the Partisan Star, third class. 5. Order of People's Liberation. 6. Order of Bravery. 7. Medal for Bravery. 8. Order of Brotherhood and Unity. I hereby request this high national forum to ratify the Supreme Command's decree of August 15, 1943, introducing military decorations into the People's Liberation Army.

The organization of our People's Liberation Army is not yet complete. We have up to the present formed eight army corps, which have all the necessary military and political personnel. But the influx of new fighters is increasing every day. New brigades and divisions are being created, and new army corps will be created. Up to the present, recruitment to our People's Liberation Army has been mainly on a voluntary basis. But now, since our people have their executive body, the National Committee of Liberation of Yugoslavia, the duty of that executive body will be to issue a decree for general compulsory military service for all citizens in the country who are between the ages of 18 and 50 years. Naturally, however, the right of any citizen outside these age limits to join the army voluntarily remains. At the same time, the National Committee of Liberation of Yugoslavia will have to make a statement about all those officers and men who are still on the side of the Germans, either in the Croatian Army or in other units.

In connection with the conference of the three great Allied powers in Moscow the time has come for our national representative body to make its view clear on a number of important questions touching the interests of our people, such as: a. the question of war criminals; b. the question of the ships, the naval and merchant vessels, which Italy seized from our people when occupying the country; c. the question of our internees in Italy and other countries; d. the question of national property looted by the Italian invaders from our people, and its return to our people. All these questions are important and pressing matters which ought to be resolved as soon as possible.

As was mentioned earlier, a delegation from the British High Command in Cairo came to the Supreme Command in May, 1943. A few days before a similar delegation landed at GHQ, Croatia. These delegations had the task of establishing contact with the People's Liberation Army of Yugoslavia and of preparing the ground for the arrival of the main delegation, headed by a British general, which is to be attached to the Supreme Command of the People's Liberation Army and Partisan detachments of Yugoslavia. The Supreme Command gave permission for such a delegation to come. And in September of this year a British military mission arrived at our headquarters. It was composed of a number of high ranking officers, headed by Brigadier F. MacLean, and had the full authority of Wilson, the Supreme Commander in the Middle East. In the credentials from the Supreme Commander, Wilson, the purpose of the mission was said to be the establishment of as close relations as possible between our People's Liberation Army and British forces, the organization of the supply of war materials to our People's Liberation Army, and the co-ordination of military operations.

Since July the Allies had been sending a certain amount of military equipment by plane, but in insignificant quantities, which was understandable, since planes were the only means of transport. With the liberation of the Dalmatian Coast and the islands the opportunity opened up of our receiving larger quantities of supplies for our army; and the Allies have in fact been sending in by boat larger quantities of military equipment and food. The prospects are that we shall receive by sea even larger quantities of the military equipment essential for the conduct of the war. Naturally, today we need heavy up-to-date equipment, like tanks and airplanes. The Supreme Command of the People's Liberation Army and Partisan detachments of Yugoslavia has already approached the Allies in this connection.

After the Supreme Command of the People's Liberation Army and Partisan detachments of Yugoslavia had established contact with the Allies, they were approached with increasing frequency by the Allies on matters which were not of purely a military character but political matters which fall within the competence of a government. On the other hand, the Supreme Command, or rather the Supreme Commander, conveyed to the Allies certain demands and requests which, in normal conditions, with a government in existence, would come within the government's competence. The Supreme Command has sent a delegation to Italy for the reception of war material, and for the organization and reception of our POWs and internees and their repatriation. Further, the Supreme Command has put its demand before the Allies for the return of naval and merchant ships which the Italians seized

from our people. It has raised the question of our internees
and prisoners. The Supreme Command has also raised the
question of supplies for our army of heavy up-to-date
equipment—tanks, aircraft, etc.—and the establishing of
naval and air bases in Italy. In this connection, the Supreme
Command of the People's Liberation Army and Partisan detachments of Yugoslavia, in agreement with the British High
Command in Cairo, has sent a delegation there to try to resolve all these questions on the spot.

All these things go to show how important and necessary it
is to set up a provisional government to resolve the majority
of these problems and to function in foreign relations as the
only legitimate and rightful representative of the Yugoslav
peoples.

The Supreme Command has succeeded in establishing contact with the Allies, that is, with Great Britain and America,
whose military representatives are in the country with us; and
now plans are being made for representatives of the Soviet
Union to come here. It is the desire of all our people, as it is
of our army, that contact be established as soon as possible
with this great fraternal state, in which the peoples of Yugoslavia have the greatest confidence, regarding it as their greatest protector.

The struggle of our peoples and the brilliant victories won
on the battlefield by our glorious People's Liberation Army
and Partisan detachments have created for us a great store of
good will among progressive people all over the world, have
created all the conditions for our peoples to realize their
aspirations—a free and truly democratic federal Yugoslavia.

IV

Address at the Third Session, Anti-Fascist Council of People's Liberation (AVNOJ)

Belgrade
August 8, 1945

The First Session of the Anti-Fascist Council of People's Liberation found Tito's Partisans isolated in Axis-occupied Yugoslavia; the Second Session found the tide of war turned against the Axis powers; and the Third Session found Yugoslavia liberated.

Following herewith is the complete text of Marshal Tito's address to the Third Session of the Anti-Fascist Council, which proclaimed itself the Temporary National Assembly of Democratic Federal Yugoslavia.

IV
Third Session of AVNOJ

Comrades: In submitting my report to this high assembly, I have considered it necessary to cover, in the briefest outline, the period from the Second Session of the Anti-Fascist Council of People's Liberation of Yugoslavia on November 29, 1943, until the present.

This has been a very significant period for our People's Liberation struggle, not only militarily but also from the political point of view.

The Second Session of the Council was held at a time when the war was raging in our country in full fury. The two great enemy offensives had just finished, the fourth and fifth offensives, which were the fiercest of all and had been conducted with the intention of destroying our People's Liberation Army and stamping out the entire Liberation movement; and the

sixth enemy offensive had already been launched. Such was
the situation at the Second Session of the Anti-Fascist Council,
which besides passing a large number of very important resolutions also set up the National Committee of Liberation of
Yugoslavia, a body which has assumed the character of a provisional government empowered to take all measures necessary for the further successful conduct of the war, for the
strengthening of the people's authorities and for insuring that
they function properly, for the organization of the economy in
liberated territory, for the defense of the achievements of the
People's Liberation struggle, for famine relief in areas liberated by the People's Liberation Army, for establishing contact
with our great Allies and seeking recognition of the existing
state of affairs in Yugoslavia, that is to say, recognition of the
People's Liberation movement and the resolutions passed at
the Second Session of the Anti-Fascist Council.

The work of the National Committee of Liberation of Yugoslavia has, naturally, been rendered more difficult on account of the fragmented character of liberated territory and its
consequent instability. The enemy has always directed his
main thrusts at the territory and location housing the Supreme
Command, and since this has usually been also the seat of the
National Committee and the Anti-Fascist Council, the enemy
has redoubled his efforts not only to dislodge us from the territory, or location, in question, but also to annihilate us. Such
was the case in the enemy attack on Western Bosnia, on Jajce
to be exact, during the sixth offensive, and on Drvar in the
seventh offensive. In these circumstances, one section of the
members of the National Committee and the Anti-Fascist
Council had to leave for the free territory in Croatia and Slovenia; and there, in spite of everything, they succeeded in doing
good work on the establishment and strengthening of people's
authorities.

It was not until after the attack on Drvar, when the Supreme Command had moved to the Island of Vis, that the Na-

tional Committee was able to reassemble on Vis and start working more effectively on its tasks.

At this time it was only the Supreme Command, and not the National Committee, that was recognized by the Allies. Consequently I, in my capacity of Supreme Commander, was able to settle many major questions with the Allies—as can be seen from this report. These questions were settled through the Allied military missions attached to the Supreme Command and also through our own missions to the Allied commands in Cairo, Italy, and, at a later date, in England. Thus, with the help of the Allies, we transported more than twenty-five thousand refugees and their children from Italy to Africa. In addition, more than ten thousand of our wounded were taken to Italy and Malta by plane (today the great majority of these refugees and wounded have been sent back home). By agreement with the Allies we set up our own military base in Bari, which, in addition to its work in organizing supplies for our military units, dealt with the matters just mentioned. The base in Bari is now in liquidation, as there is no longer any need for its existence in Italy.

THE AGREEMENT WITH ŠUBAŠIĆ

With the departure of our mission, headed by Major-General Velebit, first to Cairo and then to London, the first contact with political circles in the Allied countries was established. Through this military mission we succeeded to a large degree in acquainting the Allied public with the real facts about Yugoslavia. Besides, a meeting was arranged with Mr. Šubašić, who had been appointed by the king to form a new government in London. The meeting took place on the island of Vis on June 16, 1944, where an agreement was reached on cooperation between Mr. Šubašić's government and the National Committee, and provisions were made for three ministers from the country to enter his government.

After the meeting with Mr. Šubašić I had a meeting in

Italy with the Allied Supreme Commander, General Wilson, and other leading military figures; and on that occasion I also met Mr. Churchill. The meeting with Mr. Churchill was concerned with the speeding up of the formation of a unified government, and certain questions relating to the co-ordination of operations were also discussed. On this occasion the question of handing over the Yugoslav fleet was also settled, but unfortunately, owing to certain people who are not well disposed toward us, this agreement was not implemented until a few days ago. A few days ago the question was settled once and for all, for our representative in Italy was successful in his negotiations with the Allied military authorities in Italy in getting the Yugoslav Navy transferred immediately to our ports. It was left to the crews on the ships to decide whether to go with their ships to Yugoslavia or to remain abroad. In the latter case, the Allies have undertaken to intern them in camps.

MY VISIT TO MOSCOW

In September, 1944, I went to Moscow in order to seek help to bring about a hastening of the process of driving the occupier from our country. Since the Red Army had nearly reached the frontier of our country, it was necessary for us to reach agreement on the co-ordination of operations, and in addition I requested the Soviet Government to send Red Army troops across the frontier into Eastern Serbia to help our forces liberate Serbia and Belgrade.

The Germans at that time had very strong forces (their own and quisling forces) in Yugoslavia, with which we had been constantly engaged in bitter battles. In addition, the Germans still had strong forces in Greece and on the islands, which were due to withdraw through Yugoslavia. All this meant that the ground had to be thoroughly prepared from the military point of view, in order that our country should be liberated as soon as possible and the enemy prevented from completely destroying not only our communications but also factories and cities in the course of his withdrawal.

It was most important that we liberate Belgrade as soon as possible, thus creating conditions for the work of the National Committee and all the other military and civil authorities. This was necessary for the more effective conduct of the war and for the speedier liberation of our country. We came to an agreement that strong forces of the Red Army should cross the Danube into Eastern Serbia and together with our troops should liberate Belgrade. In addition, the Soviet Union provided a large quantity of military equipment of all kinds, from rifles to tanks and aircraft, for our army; and with this we were able to arm several of our divisions. With the help of the glorious Red Army, Belgrade and Serbia were quickly liberated; and with the help of the Bulgarian Army, Macedonia was liberated.

With the liberation of Belgrade we were in a position to carry out preparations for operations on a larger scale, for now our army, thanks to the help of the Soviet Union, was tremendously strengthened technically, and at the same time we were able to carry out conscription of new manpower.

In addition to the help just mentioned, the Soviet Union, through its river fleet, made it possible for us to supply Belgrade with fuel and provisions, so that in Belgrade lighting, water, and food were guaranteed. Finally, the Soviet Union gave us fifty thousand tons of wheat as supplies not only for Belgrade but some other areas as well.

AID FROM THE OTHER ALLIES

On the other side, our Allies Britain and America were making great efforts to supply our troops, especially in Dalmatia, Slovenia, and Bosnia. This aid was brought in by plane, usually at night. I consider it my duty to express my appreciation and gratitude to all those British and American airmen who were flying day and night, under exceedingly dangerous conditions, to supply our fighting men with military equipment and provisions. I express my appreciation to all those Soviet airmen who, with no thought for their own lives, carried military equipment day and night to our fighting men and so helped our bitter struggle.

Yes, our great Allies have helped us in our struggle, and we are grateful to them for that. It was aid well earned by superhuman efforts and sacrifices in the common Allied cause, for we carried out an unyielding fight against the occupier for two years without help from anyone. It was well justified aid, because responsible people in the great Allied countries were convinced that in Yugoslavia the People's Liberation movement was the only movement of unyielding resistance to the occupier and that everything else was a fabrication by Draža Mihailović and his like-minded friends abroad to deceive the world.

While until the liberation of Belgrade we had mainly a voluntary army, which at that time was about three hundred and fifty thousand strong, immediately after the liberation of Belgrade we went ahead with regular conscription, so that figure was doubled. We organized with the help of the Soviet Union a strong artillery, an excellent air force and tank units. All this made it possible for us in the spring of this year to launch an energetic offensive along the whole front stretching from Srem right up to Dalmatia, an energetic offensive which ended in our complete victory and in our reaching of the Soča River and the Karavanke Mountains. In this final offensive not only was the German Army smashed but also Pavelić's, which was more than two hundred thousand strong. After strong resistance a huge number of Germans and Ustashi were destroyed, and more than two hundred thousand taken prisoner, and a huge quantity of war materials was captured: thousands of lorries and field guns, every kind of military equipment, munitions, and other materials.

It is important to mention here that the enemy did not wish to capitulate or surrender even after the capitulation of Germany. Every foot of our country, right up to the frontier, had to be conquered by our troops with their blood, until the enemy forces, which wished to surrender only to the Allied forces, had been surrounded and destroyed in Slovenia.

It was a glorious and well-earned victory for our People's Liberation Army, created as it was in battle. The victory was won by an army which had been forged in the fire of battle since 1941 and had grown into a great, well-armed army, the victor and faithful guardian of the achievements for which the flower of our people laid down their lives. This army will earn gratitude from future generations for their happiness.

THE SETTING UP OF A UNIFIED GOVERNMENT

On November 1, 1944 we had another meeting with Mr. Šubašić on our territory, and we agreed on the composition of a unified government. On March 7, 1945 a unified government was formed in Belgrade; it was composed of members of the National Committee and members of Mr. Šubašić's government. In its declaration the government laid down the policy for the democratization and reconstruction of the country which up to date have been strictly carried out, as have the recommendations of the Big Three at the Yalta Conference, the best proof of which is to be found in the measures taken up to the present and in the draft laws submitted for approval to the session of the expanded Anti-Fascist Council.

The tasks in front of the National Committee after its arrival in Belgrade and in front of the unified government which was set up were formidable. Almost an entirely new state machine had to be created from scratch, because the old one had been smashed by the occupier or had been in his service. Owing to the shortage of reliable and patriotic personnel and experts the organization of the ministries and legations has not yet been completed or is not up to the standard required in particular departments for the proper performance of their functions in the interests of the state. The same is true in the governments of all the constituent republics and lower authorities, and also in many state and private undertakings. The occupier and those who were traitors to their country have left deep traces in all spheres of our social life, economic, cultural and political.

The government has been making huge efforts to eliminate all these shortcomings and to make the state machinery and the machinery of the national economy function properly. Many ill-disposed people have not understood, and still won't or can't understand, all the difficulties which this government has to face. On the contrary, these difficulties are exploited by ill-disposed people for their reactionary aims against the People's Liberation authorities and movement.

Because of the chaos created by the occupier in the monetary system, the government, in its endeavors to reconstruct economic life as quickly as possible, has had to abolish the various occupation and quisling currencies and introduce the new dinar of Democratic Federal Yugoslavia. This was—and still is—a very complicated business. In this operation there have been many shortcomings, especially in Bosnia, Croatia, and Slovenia. It might seem unfair to the constituent republics to point to these shortcomings, but they are of an objective, not of a subjective, character, and the government is trying to put matters right and it will put matters right.

Tremendous efforts have been made, with the Federal Government's help, to reconstruct our industry and get it working again and, indeed, to reconstruct our economy as a whole and our communications; and excellent results have been achieved. The best results have been achieved on the restoration of communications: on the construction of bridges and the repair of railway lines and roads. The chief credit for all these successes must go to our youth, our workers, our women, our soldiers, who have been working, often without payment, with unparalleled zeal and a desire that our country should be built up as quickly as possible from this devastation. Masses of our best patriots have worked very hard for the welfare of the whole community, and that should be an example to all those who stand on one side with their arms folded, just criticizing, while some are directly engaged in sabotage.

Great efforts have been made to provide food for the populations of the devasted areas in Montenegro, Dalmatia, Gorski Kotar, Kordun, in Bosnia and Herzegovina, in Slovenia, and elsewhere. In this we have achieved good results in spite of inadequate means of communication. Various foodstuffs and other goods essential to life, more than four hundred thousand tons, have been distributed; nearly a quarter of this was provided by UNRRA.

As a result of the serious drought in the areas mentioned, the food problem is becoming even more acute and will demand tremendous efforts if the population there is to be saved from famine. We shall have to supply these areas with essential food by winter, before the heavy snows fall, when all transport will be at a standstill. The government has also made great efforts to supply these areas with small and large livestock, and for this purpose it has advanced fifty million dinars credit for the purchase of two hundred thousand head; and one hundred thousand head of small and large livestock have already been purchased in Macedonia, Serbia, and Bulgaria. In addition, our army has placed about forty-five thousand horses at the disposal of the economy.

All this clearly shows that the state is shouldering heavy burdens and making energetic efforts to heal as quickly as possible the wounds inflicted upon us by the occupier.

REPARATIONS

Our country has been appallingly ravaged and plundered. The principal culprits responsible for all this devastation are Germany and Italy. To date they have returned nothing of what they took away and looted from our country, to say nothing of payment for war damage. To date only Hungary has begun to discharge its obligations to us, against the account of seventy million dollars reparations due to Yugoslavia. The gross figure of total damage suffered by Yugoslavia during the war is estimated at sixty-one billion dollars. Naturally, a large proportion of this falls on Italy; and for that reason one cannot help being astonished at the insolence of reactionary elements in Italy who have today shed the role of culprits and assumed the guise of accusers and slanderers of our people, when they were the ones who inflicted so much evil and devastation upon us. It is quite clear to us that those tens of thousands of men, women, and children, butchered and shot by the Italian Fascists in Slovenia, Dalmatia, Montenegro, Herzegovina, Lika, and elsewhere, can never be compensated, but the burnt-down villages and razed cities and everything that has been looted from those areas must be made good at the expense of those reactionaries; and the Italian people should see to it.

The question of payment of reparations by Germany is an urgent matter for our country. Regarding the matter realistically, our country can obtain only compensation in kind for the damage done and in such a way that our country obtain from Germany complete factories necessary for our reconstruction. Such a demand will be placed by our delegation before the Allies.

FOREIGN POLICY

Both the National Committee and the unified government have been endeavoring to get relations with our Allies on as good a footing as possible. Further, in order to eliminate everything that was prejudicial in the foreign policy of our country in the past, we are firmly determined to extend a conciliatory hand to those neighboring countries which were drawn into the war against our country by the pro-Fascist ruling circles in those countries. Last autumn, at a meeting in Craiova, I came to an agreement with Bulgarian representatives about friendship, brotherhood, cooperation and joint conduct of the war against Germany. This, our first step forward, has had good effects and has been received by our own people and by the Bulgarian people with much goodwill. Fatherland-Front Bulgaria, on its own initiative, has begun to help us in a number of ways, although the country finds itself in rather a difficult economic situation. The Bulgarian Army together with our army liberated Macedonia. All these things add daily to the strength of the brotherhood of the two countries, eliminating the gulf artificially created in the past by the reactionary rulers of Bulgaria and Yugoslavia. Today we have normal diplomatic relations and economic and cultural cooperation with Fatherland-Front Bulgaria. Further, today relations between the two countries are such that our two nations can peacefully look ahead to a happy future, assured of the realization of their age-old aspirations.

The joint struggle for freedom and the suffering shared by the Albanian people and our people have closely linked our two countries. The relations between Yugoslavia and Albania are extremely cordial and all attempts to disturb those relations are a waste of time. We were the first to recognize the democratic Albanian government and establish normal diplo-

matic relations with it. Our two countries cooperate in the
economic and cultural fields. Albania was devastated by the
occupier, and the impoverished Albanian people have earned,
with their sacrifices and their contribution to the struggle, the
maximum of goodwill and every assistance that our people
can afford, all the more so since some Albanian units, after
the liberation of Albania, joined up with our forces and
fought side by side with them to drive the enemy from Montenegro and the Sandžak. This joint struggle has forged indestructible bonds between democratic Albania and Democratic
Federal Yugoslavia.

The most significant foreign policy event in the history of
the new Yugoslavia took place on April 11, 1945, in Moscow,
with the signing of the Treaty of Mutual Assistance, Friendship, and Economic and Cultural Cooperation with the Soviet Union. This great historical act has been greeted by all
our peoples with enthusiasm. It is something they have long
and earnestly desired. But it was not until now, twenty-six
years after the creation of the old Yugoslavia, after the great
catastrophe which struck our country in 1941, after the Yugoslav peoples had taken their fate into their own hands in the
People's Liberation struggle and eliminated all those who had
hampered a rapprochement with the fraternal Soviet people
—it was not until all these things had happened that the age-
old aspirations of our people were realized and indestructible
links with the Soviet Union were established, which will be the
guarantee of our security and of great value for the development of our country.

As regards Poland, Yugoslavia was one of the first countries to welcome the Provisional Democratic Government of
Poland and establish normal relations with it. This action by
our government was joyfully received by our peoples, because
they wish to live on the best terms and in brotherly coopera-

tion with the fraternal Polish people, whose fate has been similar to our own.

With fraternal Czechoslovakia our relations have not undergone any essential change. With the liberation of Czechoslovakia they are again normal, and they will gain in strength and scope to the advantage of both countries. Work is now in progress to renew economic and cultural cooperation with fraternal Czechoslovakia, towards whom our peoples have a great store of goodwill.

With regard to our great Allies America and Britain, our country also has normal diplomatic relations with them. I believe I am expressing the thoughts of you all when I say that we wish—and we are making efforts in this direction—our cooperation and links with these two great countries to be as firm in peace as they were in war. More than that, we want them to be even more cordial. Some reactionary elements in the defeated countries are trying by means of slanders to provoke ill-feeling towards Yugoslavia on the part of our Allies. The suffering and sacrifices and the contribution of the Yugoslav peoples to the common Allied cause have been so great and incontrovertible that we firmly believe, on the basis of this, that our just demands will not be disputed at the peace conference.

With liberated France our government has now established normal diplomatic relations. Nothing stands in the way of the establishment of the most friendly relations between the freedom-loving French people and the Yugoslav people, and of cultural and economic cooperation to the advantage of both countries.

With the neighboring countries of Rumania and Hungary, which have now democratic governments, we have already established certain relations, indeed good relations, which will improve still further. The conciliatory and friendly attitude of

Yugoslavia towards the peoples of these countries, who were drawn into the war on the side of the Germans against their will, has been well received in those two countries, and it creates conditions for relations which will be a lasting guarantee that the unhappy history of the past can never happen again.

CONCLUSION

Thus, within a period of twenty months, as a result of tremendous efforts, our country can boast of fine achievements both in the battlefield and in the field of construction in the country. The greatest and most difficult task was performed by our glorious army, which at the cost of tremendous sacrifices fought for the liberation of our country and finally liberated it, with material assistance from our Allies and with material and military assistance from the glorious Red Army.

Although there are still many weaknesses, great successes have been achieved in the field of organization and strengthening of the people's authorities, especially when the very short period since the complete liberation of the country is taken into account.

With regard to the organization and operation of the state machinery, a great deal has also been done, although here there are many things that do not run smoothly and have to be put right.

With regard to the reconstruction of the country great successes have also been achieved, so that the outlook for future development is most optimistic.

With regard to the relations between our country and other states, our standing today is far better than it ever was in the old Yugoslavia. Thanks to the sacrifices made by our peoples for the common cause of victory over the enemy, today we have more friends in the world than our country has ever had.

Although our country came out of the war devastated and materially impoverished, she has at the same time undergone a spiritual renaissance and is ready for the greatest creative endeavors. A new, Democratic Federal Yugoslavia has emerged, united, in brotherhood, and at peace.

Finally, the immense sacrifices and sufferings of our peoples during the war found their reward in the greatest achievements which our peoples have ever gained: the smashing of the diabolical plan of the occupier and traitors at home to sow hatred between our peoples and prevent the creation of a strong Yugoslavia; the creation of indestructible brotherhood and unity among the various nationalities of Yugoslavia; the setting up of people's government, which is the guarantee of a just social order and democracy; and the creation of a strong state community composed of the various nationalities of Yugoslavia, all of whom have equal rights.

V

from Report to the Fifth Congress of the Communist Party of Yugoslavia

Belgrade
July, 1948

The following excerpt from Prime Minister Tito's report to the Fifth Congress of the Communist Party of Yugoslavia has dual significance: It reviews in detail the history and development of New Yugoslavia up to 1948, and it also contains an extensive rebuttal of the charges on which Yugoslavia was expelled from the Moscow-dominated world Communist movement.

V

Fifth Congress of CPY

Comrades: While the new state, the Federal People's Republic of Yugoslavia, was being created, the Communist Party of Yugoslavia had to make absolutely certain that it was a new state not only in form but also in content. It was not enough merely to carry out certain reforms, social, political and national, and then to call the new Yugoslavia a state of a new type, quite different from the old Yugoslavia. No, it was necessary to go ahead with the carrying out of fundamental changes, in the first instance economic changes, in our country, in order that it might grow and develop into a state of a new type, a Socialist state.

We did not wish to halt half way: to depose the king and abolish the monarchy, and to come to power only to share it with representatives of the capitalist class, who would continue to exploit the working masses of Yugoslavia, and so on. And the working class did not want this either, nor did the vast majority of the Yugoslav peoples. So we decided to forge boldly ahead with the complete liquidation of capitalism in Yugoslavia.

We had already created the prerequisites for this during the People's Liberation War. In all the territories where we were masters we liquidated the old bourgeois state machinery. We abolished the gendarmerie and police, and the regional, district, and urban administrative machinery. We set up new, people's authorities and their organs of security. When the country was completely liberated, we carried this out over the whole territory of Yugoslavia. Further, during the People's Liberation struggle we forged a completely new, people's army, which was not only qualitatively different from the old Yugoslav Army but was trained to serve the people and protect the building of Socialism in our country. It is an army whose chain of command, forged during the war, is composed ninety percent of workers and peasants, while the remainder are from the ranks of honest people's intelligentsia. More than ninety-four percent of the commanding personnel of our army are Communists trained by our party either during or before the war. Eighty-five thousand Communists, party members, not counting the organized youth, are today active members of the armed forces, completing their training in military skills and training new generations of soldiers, in order to preserve the independence of our country and the achievements of the great People's Liberation struggle.

Well, that is the great advantage we had, and still have, over all the other countries which have taken the road of the new type of democracy—people's democracy, because we have destroyed the old social system from its foundations and are building a new one on new foundations. And that is why the new Yugoslavia could in the immediate post-war period be called a democracy of a new type, a real people's democracy; and that is why the new Yugoslavia was able immediately after the war to go ahead with building Socialism in the country.

The vast majority of the Yugoslav people came to recognize, while the war was still in progress, that the old social system was no good, that it was outdated, and that it was necessary to create a new and better social system. That is why it was possible while the war was still in progress to forge unity among the working classes, the predominant section of the poor and medium peasantry, and the people's intelligentsia. That is why it was possible while the People's Liberation War against the occupier was still in progress to deliver a decisive blow against the pillars of the old bourgeois social system; that is why it was unnecessary after the war to settle the question of power at barricades in the streets, because the people were already holding the power firmly in their hands as the greatest achievement of the People's Liberation War against the occupier and traitors at home.

Comrades, having created, while the war was still on, the principal conditions and distinct prospects for setting up a state of a new type in place of the old one, we were unable, during the term of office of the unified government, to make any concessions to those elements in the government that were in fact representing the interests of the discarded monarchy, the bourgeoisie and their patrons abroad, in other words, international reaction. During the term of office of the unified government, that is while Šubašić, Šutej, and Grol were in it, we were subjected to great pressure from the Western Allies. Impossible concessions were sought for the bourgeois class in Yugoslavia: consistent demands were made for certain rights of the Western democratic kind, which would in effect have meant making it possible for the bourgeoisie in Yugoslavia to instigate a civil war and throw the country again into chaos

and misery. These were attempts to undermine the achievements of the People's Liberation struggle, attempts to undermine the further development of these achievements, in other
words attempts to prevent the new Yugoslavia from coming
into being.

We survived that campaign. Šubašić, Grol, and Šutej were
forced to go. While certain of the Western Allies were exerting
their pressures, we were assisted by the Soviet Union, which
gave us its full support.

Further, we were able to survive this conflict with the last
serious attempt by the reaction, for the very special reason
that we had standing behind us the vast majority of our peoples. The People's Front, under the leadership of our party,
was the mass political force which, even now, in time of peace
when it is a question of whether the old or the new will
triumph, stands as united and unswerving as it did during the
war, when it was a matter of life and death, a question of
whether our people live or die. This determination to defend
the achievements of the People's Liberation struggle was expressed by the people through their comprehensive political
organization, the People's Front, at the elections on November
11, 1945, when 96% of the electorate voted for the new Yugoslavia, thus decisively saying No to all the reactionaries who
were trying with outside help to scramble once again on to the
backs of our people.

Consequently, the unified government, which had been set
up on March 8, 1945, on outside advice, was not a monolithic government suited in all respects to the existing state of
affairs in Yugoslavia. It was only a transition period in the
process of the internal organization of Yugoslavia. And in
that period our opponents at home and abroad still had illusions about "who is going to get the better of whom." But we
suffered from no such illusions; we knew precisely how the
whole affair would end, namely, to the detriment of our oppo-

nents, to the detriment of the opponents of our peoples. We knew that cooperation could not last long, either with Šubašić, or with Grol, or with Šutej, because we had to move quickly along our clearly marked path, while they had been sent into the government to hold us up. And we were not deceived. After he had become convinced that he could do nothing to hinder us in the government, Grol resigned on August 20, 1945. Naturally, he just left, and nothing happened. After him, within two months, both Šubašić and Šutej tendered their resignations, and once again nothing happened.

They did this, on pressure from outside, on the eve of the elections for the Constituent Assembly. This was the time when reaction at home and abroad was hindering the consolidation of our country with every conceivable lie and trying in this way to prevent the elections. This was the last vigorous attempt to instigate so-called intervention by the Western powers; but this was not successful either. Šubašić and Šutej just left, like Grol before them, while the people's government remained and went full steam ahead. No, our opponents did not realize what had happened and changed in the country during the war, what profound changes had taken place in the minds of the people towards everything in the past, and so they made various unrealistic plans which were naturally doomed to failure.

With the fall of these men from the government the situation was clarified politically. The reaction had suffered another defeat and was forced to realize that there was no longer any chance of changing things here, that the working class and the working people, that is, the people's government, would not allow anyone to destroy the achievements of the People's Liberation struggle. They could see for themselves that they had only a handful of reactionaries behind them in the towns and villages, and that the whole of the working population was behind us.

On November 29, 1945, the Federal People's Republic of Yugoslavia was proclaimed by the people's representative body—the Constituent Assembly—and this decree finally abolished the Yugoslav monarchy headed by Peter Karageorgevitch and the whole Karageorgevitch dynasty.

With the enactment of the Constitution of the Federal People's Republic of Yugoslavia the edifice of state was finally completed and conditions were created for the full economic transformation of the country.

Comrades, the Constitution which was voted by the Constituent Assembly on January 31, 1946, places the achievements of our People's Liberation struggle on the statute books, and it places the national rights of all nationalities in the country and the genuinely democratic rights of all citizens on the statute books.

Let us take only Article 1 of the Constitution, which says: "The Federal People's Republic of Yugoslavia is a federal national state of republican structure, a community of peoples enjoying equal rights, who on the basis of the right to self-determination, including the right to secede, have expressed their will to live together in a federated state."

There, that is how national equality is settled here, that is how it is codified and put fully into practice.

Further, how is the question of power settled in the Constitution and in practice in this country?

In Article 6 it is stated: "In the Federal People's Republic of Yugoslavia all power derives from the people and belongs to the people. The people exercise their power through the freely elected representative bodies of state authority, from the people's committees which, from the local people's committees up to the assemblies of the people's republics and the People's Assembly of the Federal People's Republic of Yugoslavia originated and developed in the People's Liberation War against Fascism and reaction and which are the basic achievements of that struggle."

Consequently, the Constitution has only confirmed, or rather codified, what was won during the war, that is to say the power of the people, the power of a real people's democracy. This is at the same time one of the most important conditions for the further development of our country towards Socialism. This development has already progressed so far that it will be necessary at the first opportunity to make some partial amendments to the Constitution, specially in Chapter IV, on the social-economic organization of the country.

One of the important measures we had to take as early as the autumn of 1945 was the resettlement of the families of those who had fought in the People's Liberation War. This was an exceedingly difficult undertaking for us, because communications were still in ruins. About sixty thousand families of these fighting men were settled in Vojvodina, Bačka, and Slavonia, from Bosnia and Herzegovina, Lika, Kordun, Dalmatia, Montenegro, Zagorje, Serbia, Slovenia, and elsewhere. This was an immense task which demanded maximum efforts of the new state machinery, of the members of the party and front. More than four hundred and fifty thousand hectares of land, together with dwelling places and livestock, was given by the state to these settlers, and in addition we had to be responsible for seed and for helping them to cultivate the land.

Another urgent task for us was the settlement of the agrarian question. This was a question which for the twenty-four years of the old Yugoslavia's existence had been the subject of various speculative ventures by all régimes; and now it had to be settled radically.

In Article 19 of our Constitution is written: "The land belongs to those who cultivate it. The law determines whether, and how much, land may be held by an institution or a person who is not an agricultural worker. Large land holdings may not be in private hands on any grounds. The maximum size of a private holding is determined by law. The state specifically protects and assists the poor and medium peasant with its general economic policy, by cheap credits and the taxation system."

That action was taken as laid down in the Constitution is proved by the laws that were passed in connection with this. The Law on Land Reform settled this question thoroughly. Not only has all land been taken from the owners of large estates and given to the peasants, or used for the establishment of large state farms, but land of thirty hectares and more has been taken from all the rich peasants and distributed among the poor peasants. Land has also been taken from the church, a maximum of ten hectares being left but the peasants have reduced everywhere the amount of land remaining in the hands of the church.

In this way the first really heavy blow was directed against capitalist elements in the countryside, the rich men of the villages, and help given to the poor peasants. Accordingly, this is a strong proof that in the villages as well as elsewhere capitalism is being prevented from developing, that it is being continually pushed back by various state measures in favor of the poor and medium peasantry.

Naturally, no one here among the Communists, or even among a large proportion of the members of the front, harbors any illusions that we have now eliminated the danger of capitalist elements in the countryside becoming stronger. No, in this matter we have already had no small experience in a practical way, in the carrying out of various measures in the villages, such as the various collections of grain, wool, and other products, and from the resistance put up by the rich men of the villages.

This is what Lenin has to say on this matter: "Peasant husbandry continues to remain a small-scale production of goods. There we have a tremendously wide and deep-rooted basis for capitalism. On this basis capitalism conserves and restores itself in the fiercest battle with Communism. The forms of this conflict are: cheating and speculative ventures directed against the state collections of grain (and other products) and in general against the state distribution of food supplies."

Do these words not apply fully to us? They do, because they have up to now been proved completely correct in relation to conditions in our villages. But just because we know this, having learnt it from Lenin, we have taken, and will continue to take, all measures necessary to prevent these speculating, cheating capitalist elements from frustrating various state measures and impeding the growth of the Socialist sector in the countryside and threatening the building of Socialism in our country.

The third great and very important measure which we have undertaken is the nationalization of all mines, factories, and enterprises, all the means of communication, and so on; and recently additional nationalization was carried out of everything not provided for under the first Nationalization Law, as for example: the remaining industrial enterprises, all printing works, large warehouses and vaults, hotels, sanatoria, etc. In this way not only have the means of production come into the hands of the state, that is of the people, and become public property, but also all the basic public services, which have hitherto been a source of wealth to individuals—the capitalists.

This thorough nationalization and the transfer of the means of production into the hands of society has enabled us to go ahead with a planned economy, enabled us to draw up the Five-Year Plan for the industrialization and electrification of our country. All this enabled us to start putting this plan into operation in 1947; and when it has been carried out, it will completely transform the country, making it a happy and rich place.

Now we are in possession of the basic elements for building Socialism in our country. Let us once again see what these basic elements are:

1. The state authority which replaced the old bourgeois authority is a real people's government, from the lower village committees, to the highest state bodies—the federal and republican assemblies and the Federal Government and the republican governments. This authority is an expression of the will of the people, as it has been elected from bottom to top by the people, and the people can abolish it if it does not work in their interests.

2. The army is a completely new, people's army which has the task of safeguarding the peaceful development of the country, of safeguarding the achievements of the people, won in the Liberation War.

3. The state security, the militia, the UDBA, etc., are organs of the people's authority; their task is to keep a strict watch and vigil on the security of the country and its citizens and to combat any possible attempts to disturb the peaceful development of our peoples and their labors in building Socialism in our country. These organs have the job of frustrating any attempts by an enemy to inflict damage, of whatever nature, upon our country.

Consequently, we have a completely new state machinery, which is a vital condition for further development in the direction of Socialism, that is to say, the political conditions for that development have been created.

4. Radical nationalization has been carried out, so that the basic means of production have come into the hands of the people, that is of the people who work.

Thus basic material conditions, that is economic conditions, have been created for building Socialism in our country.

5. A united standpoint has prevailed among the vast majority of people, rallied in the People's Front, on all basic questions, during the common fight against the invaders and the supporters of the old social order in Yugoslavia as well as in everyday actions after the war.

Consequently the building of Socialism in Yugoslavia is the concern of the vast majority of the people, who are mobilized in the People's Front, headed by the working class and under the leadership of the Communist Party of Yugoslavia.

Comrades, the Communist Party of Yugoslavia carried out a second very important and difficult task which sprang out of the first, and it was this: the organization of the new Yugoslavia as a state was completed, but it was a state of a new type, a genuine people's democracy, founded on a federal basis, with full equality of rights for all the peoples of Yugoslavia.

Now it was necessary to proceed without delay in accomplishing the third task, an extremely difficult one—the reconstruction of the country. And our party was able to proceed with this task with such faith in success, only because of the existence of an organized force in our country known as the People's Front of Yugoslavia. Without the People's Front, which includes, as the advance guard, the whole of the working class, which includes the overwhelming majority of the working peasantry, and which includes our women, our youth, our people's intelligentsia and patriotic citizens— without this People's Front we should not have been able in such a short time to re-establish our communications, build and reconstruct our devastated villages, partially reconstruct our cities, rebuild our factories and other undertakings and get them working again (a task in which our workers have set, and are still setting, a splendid example of heroism at work); without the People's Front we should not have been able in the immediate first years to sow our fields and insure food for our population, and so on.

Here in this great and difficult task, as was the case during the war, we could see the immense energy and tenacity of our people: our workers, our glorious youth, our women, our people's intelligentsia, our working peasants, all rallied in the People's Front of Yugoslavia, that vast labor machine where all are intent on the same goal and united in their activities.

With unprecedented speed new bridges and railway lines were built, and communications, without which no major enterprise could be undertaken, were re-established. The factories, in the skilled hands of workers and experts, were quickly reconstructed and put into operation, turning out the first essential products for people in town and country. With unparalleled speed burnt-down and devastated villages up and down the land were rebuilt, rubble was cleared from cities and houses rebuilt, and so on, river and sea transport was re-established, and our fields were cultivated down to the last small patch of land. But this tremendous creative drive brought with it new and greater tasks. Our glorious youth, imbued with heroic zeal for work, demanded, and were given, the task of building the railway lines of Brčko-Banovići and Šamac-Sarajevo. These two immense projects were built by our youth in an unprecedentedly short time. They were the first priceless gifts to our young Republic—the new Yugoslavia. Our people asked not only for work on reconstruction but for new tasks, and they have carried them out with tremendous enthusiasm.

Well, this unparalleled creative drive of our people, our workers, our youth, our working peasants, members of the front, our people's intelligentsia, this was what inspired us to the decision that while reconstruction was still in progress we should tackle a tremendous undertaking—the launching of the Five-Year Plan for the industrialization and electrification of our country. It has been shown that we were not deceived in believing that even at that time, just two years after the war, it was possible to go ahead with this tremendous project.

With the fulfillment of the first year of the Five-Year Plan, it was shown that the energy of our peoples was inexhaustible, that they were aware of the tremendous significance of this undertaking for the development of our country. In a period of three years our workers raised production by leaps and bounds, while at the same time cutting costs. Our youth has given the country many precious projects, among which is the machine-tools factory at Železnik. Today they are building New Belgrade, they are building the motor highway and many other projects. Our front members are undertaking a whole host of working responsibilities, they are building cooperative centers, roads, various dwelling houses, and are doing many other important jobs in the interests of the community.

Comrades, I have only touched in passing on the results achieved in our economy, because that is the theme of reports by other comrades. I only wish to underline that we have no reason for pessimism about our capability to fulfill the Five-Year Plan. I wish to underline that we were not deceived when we decided to build Socialism in this country, because it is possible to do this; and this is confirmed by the results achieved up to now in all fields of our endeavor.

Consequently, seeing the enormous creative drive in our people and the existence of still unexploited wealth in the country, we decided, with complete faith in success, to go ahead with building Socialism in our country. This is our fourth and greatest task; and its fulfillment will make the lives of the Yugoslav people happier, richer, and much more civilized than they are today.

Comrades, at the end of my report I deem it necessary to make at least a brief mention of the Cominform resolution, of those monstrous accusations against our party and its leadership; I must mention the wild outcry and insults against our country from various quarters, in fact from where one would least expect to hear such things.

What crimes have our party and its leadership suddenly committed to have such lying accusations cast at them, accusations that are known to be lies not only by every member of our party but by every citizen in the country? Of what crimes has our country suddenly become guilty, that such a drastic campaign has been launched against it? Let us see what is involved. Is there really some valid reason for adopting such an attitude towards our party and its leadership, towards our country and its people? Is it possible that because of the accusations in the Cominform resolution, even supposing them to be true, our country and its peoples can be affronted by such appalling slanders by the very countries with which we have, not just normal relations, but allied friendly relations?

This, comrades, is not just an attack on the leadership of our party. It is an attack on the unity of our party, it is an attack on the unity of our peoples purchased at the price of so much blood, it is a call to all the destructive elements to smash everything that we have built up to now for the happiness of our people; it is a call to civil war in the country, a call for the destruction of the country.

We consider the bitterest pill in that resolution the accusation that we turned our backs on the Soviet Union and the countries of people's democracy, that we are nationalists and not internationalists, that we have renounced the teachings of Marxism-Leninism. I shall answer only these three accusations.

First, in our foreign policy since the war we have gone hand in hand all the way with the foreign policy of the Soviet Union, for the simple reason that it is a policy which has been, and still is, in keeping with the interests of our country and the interests of peace in the world. Our standpoint is known to the whole world, because everything has been written down or delivered in numerous speeches, both at international conferences and in this country as well. And our standpoint, that is, loyalty and solidarity with the Soviet Union and the other countries of people's democracy on foreign policy questions, has not been confined to words but has been expressed in deeds, as is well known, not only to every citizen of this country but to our friends and enemies throughout the world.

The first foreign policy measure taken by the Central Committee of the Communist Party of Yugoslavia and our government after the war was to insure that Yugoslavia's ties, economic, political, and cultural, with the Soviet Union and the countries of people's democracy, should be as close as possible. The contracting of pacts of friendship and mutual assistance, comprehensive cooperation, and the conclusion of various economic and other agreements, was done on our initiative, and no one drove us to it. We considered that this was in fact the most appropriate thing to do for the peaceful development of our country, for the cementing and preservation of peace in the world, and also for the strengthening of democracy in other countries—such as Poland, Czechoslovakia, Bulgaria, Hungary, and Rumania. As for Albania, we concluded a pact on mutual assistance, friendship and comprehensive cooperation with her, precisely in order to help her preserve her independence. We concluded economic agreements with Albania, which were, in the main, to the disadvantage of Yugoslavia; but we concluded them because we did not wish Albania to become ever again a tool for any kind of attempt to exploit and threaten her independence. So, we have been giving Albania every possible assistance at a time when it has been most needed, in other words, right from the end of the war up to the present time.

We have, right up to the present, remained faithful to all our obligations towards the countries of people's democracy. But, on the other hand, we have emphasized the need for cooperation with other countries too, for we considered this to be conducive to cementing peace in the world, and we considered it to be in the interests of Yugoslavia, which had suffered so terribly in the great Liberation War. But this never exceeded the boundaries of strict preservation of our principles of loyalty to Marxism and loyalty to our friends—the USSR and the countries of people's democracy. In this connection I must emphasize that we were the ones, that is Yugoslavia was the country, most fiercely slandered and attacked by the whole group of international reactionaries because of its unswerving stand in foreign policy matters, which was in every respect in line with the foreign policy of the countries of people's democracy and the USSR. Our stand is known, not only to every citizen of this country but to the whole world. Consequently, a terrible injustice is being done to us, that is to our country, when we are accused of isolating ourselves from the front of democracy.

Further, those who are attacking us today, and they are the leaders of the Communist parties of the very countries to which we have given most assistance, should at least have the honesty not to make use of such appalling, fabricated slanders, such as that we are nationalists, that is, that we are no longer internationalists, and so on. Is the waiving of twenty-five million dollars reparations due to be paid by the fraternal Bulgarian Republic, the waiving of payment for most of the national property looted by Bulgarian Fascists in Yugoslavia, is the extending of a brotherly hand to the people of Bulgaria, thus burying all the past—is that nationalism? No, no one in the world can say that is nationalism. It is something quite different, something profoundly international, something human and unselfish to the point of self-sacrifice, something prompted by the desire that the material sacrifices made by war-stricken Yugoslavia, made by our peoples for Bulgaria, should be an earnest that all the evils done to them by the Bulgarians in the past are forgotten, and that they offer, not only a brotherly hand, but also material support to the fraternal Bulgarian people. That was the policy of brotherhood and forgiveness pledged before our people by the leadership of the Communist Party of Yugoslavia, which today is being so shamefully slandered and smeared by the leaders of the Communist Party of Bulgaria.

Further, it is a well-known fact that in 1946 we had a serious drought and a poor harvest but that nevertheless we complied with a request from our Rumanian comrades and gave them two thousand carloads of grain at a time when their people were dying of hunger, although the food situation among our own population was serious at the time. We laid down no conditions, nor did we ask when this would be paid back, but we left the matter and waited two years until they had a good harvest, and then they began to pay us back. This grain was given by our party leadership, that is by our government, at the expense of our own working people. But our working people willingly gave to those whose need was greater. Is that nationalism? It is internationalism put into practice, not merely into words.

We acted in the same way towards Poland in 1947 and towards Czechoslovakia, giving them more than 15,000 carloads of grain, although our own people almost went hungry that year. We gave because they asked us, because they were in an even more critical situation than we were.

And what are the representatives of those countries doing today, at Cominform meetings, signing a resolution pharisaically accusing us of conducting wrong policies in respect of food supplies for our population? They speak of some sort of grain tax here, and so on, which is just an ordinary delusion of people abroad, because everyone here knows that there is no such thing as a grain tax here, that it has never been introduced in this country. We have various difficulties which result from the devastation of the war—and they exploit these to slander our party and the Central Committee of our party. The signatories (of the resolution) do not want to see that we could not possibly overcome these difficulties in such a short period, that is, in the three years since the war. They have done less to overcome their difficulties, although these were much less severe than ours. Nevertheless, they maliciously impute to us things that have no basis. They forget that in the year 1921–1922 the leadership of the Soviet Union, headed by Lenin, was forced to introduce NEP, the new economic policy as it was called, because, among other things, of the difficulties that existed in supplying the population of the Soviet Union with food, and that there were still great difficulties in that respect in the Soviet Union in 1929. Then why do they suddenly refuse to admit that we have difficulties in front of us? Is that not the ultimate disloyalty on the part of the signatories of the resolution? And, on the other hand, does not the aid that we extended at a time when we were faced with difficulties ourselves amount to internationalism, internationalism in practice, and not in phrases, in words? And do these people who are now falsely and unjustly attacking us not think that one day they will have to blush for shame when they are asked by their people why they did not tell the truth?

For these people nationalism is the fact that we are proud of our sacrifices in the war, that we are proud of our successes in building up the country, that we are proud of our workers, our youth, our People's Front, that we are proud of all the things that have captured the admiration of all honest people in the world. That's what they call nationalism. But no, it is not nationalism. It is an irrefutable fact that no one can deny, something of which we can be really proud. Can we really renounce everything and say that we are nationalists, merely because that is what has been alleged in the Cominform resolution? It goes without saying that we cannot admit that the facts here that tell a different story are not facts, while what is written in the resolution is the truth. We cannot admit such a thing, merely because it has been written down and signed in the Cominform resolution. The signatories have taken no account whatever of the objective truth. They consider their behavior, not only to the Central Committee of the Communist Party of Yugoslavia but also to Yugoslavia as a whole, that is, their attitude to facts which prove the objective truth, to be Marxist-Leninist behavior. Quite the contrary: it is not Marxist-Leninist! The truth is that it is at best disloyal and unobjective behavior towards our party and the country. It is the result of a terrible blunder. Now the whole thing has been blown up to monstrous proportions, in order to destroy the respect enjoyed by our party and its leaders and to strip the Yugoslav peoples of their glory in their heroic struggle, in order to trample under foot all the great things our peoples have achieved by the tremendous sacrifices and by the rivers of blood they have shed, in order to destroy the unity of our party, which is the guarantee for the successful building of Socialism in our country and the creation of a happier life for our people.

Comrades, I am not now going to enter upon a long diatribe against the Cominform resolution, which is full of untruths. That is known to everyone in this country, because everyone here knows what is the truth and what is not. Everyone in this country knows that capitalism cannot spread in this country, but that on the contrary Socialism is being built and at a pretty quick rate. Everyone, not only here but outside the country as well, knows that in the post-war period we have achieved tremendous successes in building up the country. Every member of our party, and not only every member of our party but every citizen in the country as well, knows the legal status of our party, a status which it won, rifle in hand, in the great Liberation War against the occupier and those who had driven the party underground in 1921.

Comrades, there was no difficulty for anyone to recognize the contradictory nature of the formulations in the Cominform resolution. On the one hand they accuse us of being opportunists, of allowing the growth of capitalism in the countryside, of considering the peasantry as a whole to be the main factor in the building of Socialism, of taking a line leading to the restoration of capitalism, in other words, of turning the new Yugoslavia into a bourgeois state, and so on, while on the other hand they accuse us of oppressing the peasants and ordering them about—as some of these super-Marxists now write. In a word, all kinds of things are fabricated, just to make the confusion among their own people all the greater, since they are unable to convince them of the truth of their unfounded accusations. Further, it is asserted that we are building Socialism too quickly, that we pass laws and issue edicts overnight, and so on. And, finally, the charges they level against us are the same as those once levelled by Milan Grol and the rest of the reaction in our country and outside it.

It is strange that they should level the charge against us in the resolution that we concealed from the masses the criticism of our leadership by the All-Union Communist Party (b), and they attributed as our reason that we were afraid for ourselves because of the masses. No, we had no fear for ourselves to publish it, we were afraid it might cause even more bitterness against those who accused us unjustly. The signatories of the resolution know very well that we were unable to publish a letter sent by the Central Committee of the All-Union Communist Party (b) which was marked "strictly confidential." Nevertheless, these signatories now lay the blame for this on us.

Comrades, if those who are thus accusing us wanted to succeed in blackening us in the eyes of the proletariat of other countries, and in smearing our country, our leadership, and our party, then they have only had a partial success and one that will not last for long. The truth must prevail, because the truth consists of irrefutable facts which cannot be hidden for long from the proletariat of other countries. Besides, the majority of the men who participated in framing the accusations in the resolution represent countries whose development since the war lags far behind Yugoslavia's. Would it not be wiser if these critics criticized themselves and their own work, because shortcomings and mistakes of every shape and form exist in abundance in their countries. But perhaps that is just why they found it necessary to smear our leaders, our party, and our country?

Comrades, attempts are now being made on all sides to teach us the ABC of Marxism-Leninism; and the teachers are storming open doors and extracting quotations from the works of Marx, Engels, Lenin, and Stalin, without taking into consideration the fact that we have for a long time been putting these quotations to practical account, and we are still doing so. They now refuse to admit that we are Marxists and Leninists. But on the basis of what teaching could we, that is, our party, achieve such tremendous successes? Did we in 1941 enter the life-and-death struggle on the side of the Soviet Union on the basis of Trotskyist conceptions? Or was it because of loyalty to Marxism-Leninism, the theory which the Soviet Union is endeavoring to put into practice? Logic says that we entered the struggle because we were Marxist-Leninists, not only in words but in deeds.

The tremendous role of the Yugoslav Communist Party in the Liberation War and its triumph over all difficulties has been the result only of the fact that we have conducted ourselves and have known how to orientate ourselves on the basis of the teachings of Marxism-Leninism. Consequently, to create such unity in a party such as ours, such a glorious party as ours, to solve the national question in the way that we have done, to create such national unity and brotherhood as we have done

in Yugoslavia, to wage a Liberation War under the most difficult conditions and emerge victorious, to build all that we
have built since the war and then to go forward with building
Socialism in our country—these things can only be achieved
by a nation that is led by a party of steel such as our Communist Party, can only be achieved by a party which is familiar
with the laws of social development and conducts itself according to the teachings of Marxism-Leninism.

When after all we have achieved—and they are real
achievements—it is contested that we have in a certain sense
blazed a new trail, that means proclaiming Marxism-Leninism
as a dogma, something which does not lend itself to further
development whatever new conditions may arise. This is undi-
alectical; and on this point we hold to the teachings of Lenin
who, in a quotation from Engels, said: "Our teaching, Engels
was speaking here on behalf of himself and his eminent comrade" [Marx, interposed Tito], "is not a dogma but a guide to
action." Lenin goes on: "In this classic passage a side of
Marxism which is nearly always overlooked is emphasized
with splendid clarity and strength. But by overlooking it we
make Marxism one-sided, distorted, dead. We remove its living
soul, we extirpate its basic theoretical roots—dialectics, the
teaching on the subject of historical development which is
comprehensive and full of contradictions: we disrupt its ties
with the specific practical tasks of a given epoch, which may
change with every new turning point in history. . . ." And
further on Lenin says: "And in our own day one very often
comes across people with an interest in the future of Marxism
in Russia who neglect that particular side. However, it is clear
to everyone that in recent years Russia has experienced extremely serious upheavals which have with remarkable speed
and acuteness changed the situation, the social-political situation, which determines in the nearest and most direct manner
the conditions for action, and consequently the tasks of the

activity. . . . Precisely because Marxism is not a dead dogma, not a complete, ready-made, immutable doctrine, but a living guide to action, that is precisely why it cannot do otherwise than reflect on itself the appallingly sharp changes of conditions in social life. . . ." [Lenin: *Sochineniya,* Book XV, "Regarding some peculiarities in the historical development of Marxism."]

Well, that is what Lenin said and taught, while they want to compel us to keep strictly to a certain formula on our road to building Socialism.

Comrades, since the question is, have there or have there not been mistakes in our party work, then, naturally, no one in our party will assert that there have not been any. It is well known that we are relentless in castigating our mistakes, not only inside the party, but in public, in front of the whole population of the country. We have never been ashamed to admit our mistakes, which have been made, are still made, and will probably continue to be made; but we are endeavoring, and we must continue to endeavor, to insure that there are as few as possible in the party. From day to day we discover our mistakes and try to correct them. Sometimes we put matters right quickly, sometimes more slowly; but they are mistakes of quite a different character from those which are imputed to us. We ourselves can see our own mistakes, the members of our party can see them and so can the people's masses, because they are mistakes bound up with matters of everyday life. They often give us a bad time, because sometimes we do not discover them, do not see them in time. But what party is immune from error? There is no party, there is no man who works and never makes a mistake.

The charge is leveled against us that here there is neither criticism nor self-criticism. This is ignorance of the state of affairs here. Let these critics, the signatories to the resolution, just read any of our speeches or articles, and they will see immediately that they have gone too far in their accusations. Precisely because we realize the significance of criticism and self-criticism for a revolutionary party, we have succeeded in creating such a monolithic party as ours. And that is precisely why our party has been able to triumph over all difficulties and achieve in practice the best results after those of the All-Union Communist Party (b).

Comrades, the false accusations in the Cominform resolution and the slanderous campaign abroad against our party and the country as a whole have subjected our party to a severe ordeal, the most severe ordeal in its history. No other Communist Party, with the exception of the All-Union Communist Party (b), would be able to withstand such onslaughts without immediately falling to pieces like a house of cards. Naturally, this great ordeal will make a clean sweep of all those in the party who do not belong in such a steeled party as ours. They are individuals, waverers and weaklings, hostile elements, who have up to now camouflaged themselves in the party, people like, for example, Žujović and Hebrang. Usually such people raise their heads at times when things are most difficult for the party, and in various ways come out openly against the party, thinking that the time is ripe for them. Such people usually fall, and will inevitably fall, from the chariot of the revolution, because they are detrimental not only to our party and our country but to the further development of Socialism as a whole. In this matter we shall remain unrelenting and consistent, as we have learned to be from Marx, Engels, and Lenin.

Comrades, I have endeavored in this rather long report to make our younger cadres better acquainted with the development and work of the Communist Party of Yugoslavia, so that they will get to know its weak and its positive sides. If I have succeeded, among other things, in showing what a tremendous part unity plays in our party's successes, then I have done well, for it was only the destruction of factions and the creation of indestructible unity in our party that enabled it to become the true avant-garde of the working class and to stand in 1941 at the head of a subjugated Yugoslavia and to conduct the Liberation struggle to victory over the occupier and traitors at home. This unity has in the past been the guarantee of all victories which have a historical significance, and this is so outside the frontiers of our country, as well. But this unity is not the ordinary unity which may exist in other parties, even Fascist ones. It is not unity for the sake of unity, for the sake of God's peace or some discipline which is an aim in itself. No, it is the revolutionary unity of a revolutionary party, which enables the avant-garde of the working class to carry through its revolutionary mission. Consequently, we must safeguard the unity of our party from all onslaughts, because it is the guarantee of the victory of Socialism in our country.

Once again today our party is threatened by a great danger from various undercover anti-party elements, which at the instigation of the Cominform have raised their heads to threaten the unity of our party. But this time these anti-party elements are endangering not only the unity of the party but also the unity of the peoples of this country. Consequently, this compels us to be implacable against all attempts to disrupt the unity of our party and the unity of our peoples. The unity of our party is inseparable from the brotherhood and unity of our peoples and consequently the responsibility falling on us, members of the Communist Party of Yugoslavia, is all the greater. For this reason, comrades, let us be implacable against all deviations in our party, let us preserve its unity and purity, let us master as completely as possible the science of Marxism-Leninism, let us foster the basic qualities of Communists—criticism and self-criticism, as one of the strongest weapons of Communists in their daily task of correctly carrying out the party line!

Finally, comrades, I would emphasize that our party and our Central Committee will do all in their power to insure that relations between our party and the All-Union Communist Party (b) are again improved. We hope that the leaders of the All-Union Communist Party (b) will give us the opportunity of proving, here, on the spot, all that is incorrect in the resolution. We consider that only in this case and in this way can the truth be established.

In concluding my report, comrades, I must emphasize that up to now the Communist Party of Yugoslavia has honorably fulfilled its historical mission and will, I am fully convinced, continue to fulfill it honorably by winning the victory of building Socialism in our country, and that it will by its steadfastness and unity and its unwavering faith in the science of Marx-Engels-Lenin prove conclusively that it has not deviated from the path of that science.

VI

On Workers' Management in Economic Enterprises

Belgrade
June 26, 1950

Of all the social, economic, and political innovations of New Yugoslavia, none has attracted more worldwide attention than the institution of workers' councils. The following excerpt from his Report to the National Assembly presents Prime Minister Tito's comments at the time of the enactment of the law implementing the new system of economic management.

VI

Workers' Management in Economic Enterprises

Comrade People's Deputies: As I said earlier the law which we are to adopt here is of great importance for the future correct development of our Socialist country, but it still does not settle this question completely; it is merely another step forward towards Communism. The functions of the state in the administration of the economy have not yet completely ceased, but they are no longer exclusive. They are diminishing as the result of workers being drawn into management. The workers are beginning to take up their right as producers to manage production, but gradually, not all at once. Why is this happening gradually, and not all at once? Will this take a long time, and if so how long? One cannot tell how long this will take, because it depends on various circumstances. It depends on the speed of cultural development, that is, the all-round training of the workers to make them capable of carrying out the management of factories, mines, transport, etc., efficiently and for the benefit of the community, because otherwise the workers will not be able to exercise supervision and control. Without a rise in their educational standards workers will not be able to acquire complete mastery over the technique of management. And that, again, depends on the speed of development of the productive forces, etc.

A rise in the cultural level of workers is all the more important to us, and is one of our most difficult problems, because our country used to be one of the most backward countries in Europe in respect of the level of productive forces. Our industry has now begun to go full steam ahead with its development. Consequently, the transfer, sooner or later, of all functions of management in the economy to the workers depends in our country on the higher or lower rate of development in productive forces. This depends, first of all, on the workers themselves, on their determination to produce as many consumer goods as possible, as quickly as possible, on the efforts made by workers to save, and not to squander, and so on.

Lenin says: "Communism begins where ordinary workers are showing an unselfish determination, overriding the hardships of their labor, to achieve an increase in the productivity of labor, and to insure that every pood of grain, coal, iron, and other products, is conserved, not for their own benefit, not for the benefit of those close to them, but for the benefit of people more remote—that is, society as a whole."

Why am I stressing, as first priority, the need for educational development? If we look at the number of industrial workers there were in the old Yugoslavia, then at the number today and the number there will be in the future, it is not difficult to see the reason for that. Who are the people today entering industrial and other enterprises? The peasants. The point is, an enormous number of peasants, or people who are half-peasants half-workers, are now coming into the enterprises, and they have to be trained as workers, and then educated as worker-managers. This is no easy, short-term task, and it must be tackled with the greatest resolution and patience and energy, until it is mastered. In the training of these new workers we shall have, as we already have at the moment, a considerable job with the strange ideas that prevail among many of these workers about their duties, and about their relation to the state's, that is, the people's property, and so on.

Let us just take the fact that we are building and opening up many projects, even certain major factories, mines, and the like, right in the most economically backward parts of the country, like parts of Bosnia, the Sandžak, Macedonia, Kosovo-Metohija, Lika, Montenegro, and so on, in other words in all sorts of places where previously there has been very little industry or hardly any at all. Who is going to work in those factories, mines, and other enterprises? The peasants from those backward areas. The poor peasants from those backward parts of the country will have to go into the factories and mines, and they will. They have to change from poor peasants, whose ancestors have for centuries scraped a living on the lowest standard and at the lowest cultural level, into enlightened workers, builders of a better life for themselves and the whole of the Socialist community. This will be no easy and rapid process, we are aware of that, for today we have enough experience of the difficulties of turning a half-peasant half-worker into an enlightened and disciplined industrial worker. To achieve this great efforts are needed; no pains must be spared to show these half-workers that in our Socialist country they are becoming not merely producers in industry, the mines, and so on, but also owners of the means of production; they have to be shown that by entering the factories, mines, and so on, they become the actual owners. Not that little plot of infertile ground which could never provide them with a substance worthy of a man, but factories, mines, and so on, can insure for them a better life than they or their forebears ever had. Why is there a need for these half-peasants half-workers to become enlightened industrial workers? It is necessary first of all because we are building numerous factories and enterprises, we are opening up an increasing number of new mines, in a word, we are industrializing our Socialist country in order to make it richer, in order that its unexploited wealth shall be available to all citizens of our country, in order that people can avail themselves of this wealth, and so on. In order to get the factories, mines, and so on, started, workers are needed who are capable of mastering the latest techniques and getting them under way. These up-to-date techniques cannot be handled by the semi-peasant, who thinks more of his plot of infertile ground than of the latest modern means of production, which are now no longer private, capitalist property, but the social property of our entire community. They are no longer managed by the capitalists or their well paid faithful officials, the bureaucracy, which only looked after the interests of the capitalists with a view to insuring that as much profit as possible was squeezed out of the workers for the capitalist pocket, at the same time receiving a few crumbs for itself. Today in this country the factories, mines, and the like are going to be managed by the workers themselves. They themselves will determine the methods and volume of work, they will know why they are working, and the purposes for which the results of their labor will be used. In order that this may be carried out throughout the country, even in the most backward parts, a ceaseless struggle will have to be waged against backwardness, and the level of the semi-peasants will have to be raised to that of enlightened industrial workers who understand their rights and duties as builders of Socialism.

From all this it will be seen that there are tremendous difficulties in the way of building Communism in a backward country, such as ours for example. But what next? Shall we wait until the workers are all equally clever and capable of managing enterprises? Obviously not, because in that case we would have to wait an unconscionably long time. In the actual process of management, in the ceaseless process of work and management, all the workers will acquire the necessary experience. They will get to know not only the work process but all the problems of their enterprise. It is only by practice that the workers can learn to use the production index, thus getting to know how much material can be used and how much can be economized, getting to know all the uses to which the results of their work are put, that is, where their surplus labor goes and to what use it is put. They must get to know what level of accumulation their enterprise must achieve as its share of the general planned accumulation, and how much they can increase their standard of living with the remaining output surplus. They must get acquainted with the level and rate of increase which they must achieve in labor productivity, and so on. It is absolutely essential that they get to know all about working discipline, because from the moment that the workers take over the responsibility of participating in the management of the economy, then the problem of working discipline will be among their principal duties.

It will be of particular importance for the councils of the working collectives to use their influence to insure as rational a distribution of labor as possible, so as not to allow unproductive labor to become ensconced in their enterprises, that is to say, a top-heavy bureaucracy in the administration, because this is a sure way of increasing production costs and reducing the profitability of their enterprises, which will do harm to the entire collective. It is necessary to know how to distinguish between the need for specialists and a top-heavy, unproductive administrative machine.

The transfer of the factories and mines, etc., to management by workers' collectives will prevent the infectious disease known as bureaucracy becoming endemic in our economy. This disease is carried with incredible ease and rapidity from bourgeois society and it is dangerous in the transitional period, because like a squid with a thousand tentacles it holds back and hampers the correct process and the speed of development. Bureaucracy is among the greatest enemies of Socialism for the reason that it is drawn in unnoticed at every pore of social activity, without people being aware of it at first. It would be wrong to imagine that bureaucracy has not begun to take root here. It has already begun to insinuate itself into various institutions, into the state machinery and the economy, but we are aware of it, and so we have taken a whole range of measures to prevent it. Spasmodic campaigns are not sufficient; what is needed are unceasing efforts and the education of the people.

Lenin says that cultural and technical backwardness is the most favorable soil for bureaucracy to take root, but he also tells us the easiest way, or rather the only possible way, to fight against bureaucracy.

> A fight to the finish against bureaucracy, and complete victory over it, will only be possible if the entire population has a share in the administration. In bourgeois republics, this not only has been impossible, but the law itself is a stumbling block. The best bourgeois republics, however democratic, have thousands of legal snags which prevent workers from having a share in the administration. We have taken measures to insure that such snags do not exist with us, but so far we have not been able to insure the working masses their share in the administration—apart from the law there is also the cultural level which cannot be subordinated to any law. This low cultural level makes the Soviets, which on the basis of their program ought to be administrative bodies acting through the working people, in fact administrative bodies for the working people, acting through the most progressive layer, the proletariat, and not through the toiling masses.*

* Lenin, *Works,* Volume XXIV, page 145, third Russian edition.

This was because of the cultural backwardness of which Lenin was speaking, and herein lies the danger of the bureaucratization of the administration.

According to Lenin, it can be seen that bureaucracy flourishes particularly where there is a greater degree of backwardness. These words make it quite plain where we must seek the roots of bureaucracy. Does not this show that bureaucracy flourishes precisely where people are not aware of their right to control, and to wage a decisive struggle against every bureaucratic procedure, where people are not yet aware that the presence of bureaucracy is detrimental to Socialism, and it cannot be extirpated merely by decrees from above, but every conscious individual should fight against it in his everyday life. It should not be imagined that bureaucracy can only prevail in the higher institutions and that it is more difficult for it to prevail on a lower level. No, bureaucracy penetrates to a lower level too, down to the lowest state and economic administrative institutions, if we do not fight against it. It goes without saying, it is a tragedy for a Socialist country if bureaucracy takes root in the administration from top to bottom, if the people at the top do not, or will not, see the harm it can do. In order to counter bureaucracy successfully, it is not enough to take measures against it only on a top level, on the highest official level, and to consider, on a lower level, that it is, allegedly, not dangerous. How really dangerous it is on lower levels practical experience has shown us. Consequently, bureaucracy is a danger, whether in the administration of the republics, or in the administration of the regions, or in the administration of the districts and local bodies, or in the administration of the various commercial and other economic institutions; and it is imperative that we enlist the assistance of the broadest masses to fight against it and not allow this menace to Socialism to get under way.

Today, when not only the state administration but the en-

tire economy is in the hands of the people, the people are
competent to exercise a vigilant supervision over the work of
those who are placed in the administration to carry out their
duties for the benefit of the Socialist community. The working
collectives and their councils, which are going to manage the
factories and mines, etc., will have a very important task in
preventing bureaucratic methods in the management.

THE ROLE OF THE TRADE UNIONS

The role of the trade unions under the new conditions, under
the conditions in which the workers have a share in the management of the economy, is changing in some respects, for the
function of the unions now is mainly directed towards what is
most important in the work of a trade union—education, and
a general raising of the cultural level of the workers. The
work of the unions is directed towards insuring that the newly
arrived workers, formerly peasants, rid themselves, with the
help of the tireless work of the unions, and under the leadership of the party, as soon as possible of their old small-holder
mentality, that they reach in as short a time as possible the
level of the most enlightened industrial workers, workers with
a new, Socialist attitude towards the means of production, towards the factories, towards the mines, towards social property, and towards work. These new workers must be trained
as soon as possible to be tireless and self-sacrificing builders of
Communist society, that is, of a better and happier life for all
working people.

In view of the participation of the workers in the management of enterprises, or rather of production generally, their
former task of safeguarding the interests of the workers is in
decline, because this is a matter which the workers settle for
themselves through their councils, or through the boards of
management in industry. This at the same time eases the dual
role of the unions, which had on the one hand to protect the

interests of the workers and on the other to take account of the interests of the people's state, the interests of the whole, the entire community. By getting the workers acquainted, in the process of managing production, with all its problems— with accumulation, production costs, numerous difficulties of all kinds which were hitherto tackled by the directors themselves or the former managements and the trade unions respectively—the work of the trade unions will be eased in this respect. In any case it will help to stabilize working discipline in the factories, mines, and other enterprises.

It can be seen from the law that the workers are taking up their functions in management in a most democratic fashion. The workers' councils are elected, directly, by a secret ballot of the workers and employees in factories, mines, and enterprises generally. These workers' councils and boards of management, which are elected by the members of the councils among themselves, must have the complete support of the trade unions. To make this possible members of the workers' and employees' trade union in the enterprise are included in the board of management and in that way they bear their share of the responsibility for management, instead of being merely consultative bodies without any particular responsibility, or rather, responsible duty.

This law is among the most democratic laws adopted by us so far; in its content it reflects our Socialist reality. Let us take just the duties and rights of the workers' councils. It is stated in Article 23:

"The workers' council of an enterprise:

approves the basic plans and the final account of the enterprise;

passes resolutions for administering the enterprise and for fulfilling the economic plan;

elects, dissolves, and replaces the board of management or its individual members;

passes the regulations of the enterprise with the assent of the board of management or the higher economic association or the competent state body;

debates the work reports of the board of management and passes resolutions approving its work;

debates the individual measures of the board of management and passes resolutions concerning them;

effects the allocation of that part of the accumulation which is at the disposal of the enterprise, that is to say, of the working collective."

Further on in Article 27, it is stated in respect of the duties of the board of management:

"The board of management of an enterprise:

elaborates proposals for the basic plans of the enterprise;

introduces the monthly operational plans;

is responsible for the proper running of the enterprise;

makes recommendations for the internal organization of the enterprise and recommendations for the classification of jobs;

makes recommendations for regulations governing work routines and introduces measures for tightening work discipline;

appoints employees to executive posts in the enterprise;

makes decisions after hearing workers' and employees' complaints about dismissals and internal work schedules;

takes measures for promoting production in the enterprise, particularly for rationalizing production, increasing labor productivity, reducing production costs, improving the quality of products, making economies, and reducing wastage and rejects;

settles questions relating to norms in the enterprise;

approves the nomination of shock-workers and recommendations for rationalization methods and innovations;

takes measures for raising the level of skill among workers

and employees in the enterprise, and also for insuring a proper system of assigning workers to jobs;

is responsible for the correct interpretation of the regulations governing labor relations in the enterprise, for wages, salaries, for the promotion of workers and employees, for safety measures at work and social insurance, and also for improving the living conditions of workers and employees in the enterprise;

approves the rota for workers' and employees' annual holidays;

takes measures for the protection and proper utilization of the public property managed by the enterprise and measures to ascertain, prevent, and eliminate harmful practices, wastefulness, and other manifestations of an unconscientious attitude towards public property.

The board of management of the enterprise is responsible for the fulfillment of the plan and for the proper running of the enterprise."

These two articles of the law explain how all functions in industry are now transferred to the working collectives, functions which hitherto have been fulfilled by the state and exercised through its appointed representatives, with a certain measure of trade union participation.

Now, however, state ownership of the means of production, the factories, mines, and railways, is gradually changing into a higher form of Socialist ownership. State ownership is the lowest of social ownership, not the highest, as the leaders of the USSR imagine.

Well, therein lies our path towards Socialism, and it is the only right way since it is a matter of the withering away of the functions of the state in the economy. Let the Cominformists bear in mind that their slanderous uproar cannot darken our well-lit path of building Socialism.

On the other hand, this law on the participation of the

work collectives, that is the workers themselves, in the management of the economy of the country, is the most effective answer to the question of where true democracy is to be found: Here, in this country, or in the much boasted and praised democracy of the West. With us democracy is founded on a material basis for the benefit of the broadest masses of working people. The masses of people feel this democracy, they employ it to create a better and happier future for all the working people of our country. That is the answer to those in the West who talk so much about there being no genuine democracy in this country, who say that it is a police state, who like to dwell on our shortages, saying that we lack this and that and so on. Well, there are still great shortages here in many things, for we are not yet in a position to build up sufficient resources, to produce sufficient goods for our needs, sufficient of all the things that make life easier for people and raise their standard of living. But we are now well on the way to achieving this, and we shall do so for the good of everyone, not just for a minority, as is the case in the West. What use is it in the West if the stores are full of everything that man's heart desires? For how many people there can satisfy those desires? It goes without saying that only a small fraction, only the ruling class, is in a position to do that, and not the vast majority of the working people. Consequently, it is only a democracy for a minority, since the working people, who barely scrape a livelihood, or the unemployed industrial and clerical workers, get nothing out of such a democracy which takes the fruits of their labor away from them and only tolerates them in order that they may support others who are quite fit physically and are thus secured a rich and comfortable life. We, however, work on the basis that those who work should enjoy the fruits of their labor; and therein lies the material basis of our democracy.

We are aware that we shall have our share of trouble before

the workers finally overcome all the difficulties arising from our backwardness; but we can be sure that our workers will triumph over these difficulties, because they are aware that building Socialism is their personal concern and can only be achieved as the result of their own persistent, self-sacrificing, creative zeal.

From the very outset our people's authorities have paid the greatest attention to the welfare of the workers, of the people of our country, for they would not be people's authorities if they acted differently. Everything built and accomplished in this country has one aim: to bring happiness to our workers, to create better living conditions for them. The workers in town and country are themselves the masters of their present and their happy future. How soon this happy day will come, the day when it will no longer be necessary for people to work so hard, depends on the workers themselves in town and country, depends on their determination, self-sacrifice, and patience; it depends on their sparing no efforts, on there being as few people as possible who stand and look on, and on insuring that everyone makes a major effort in the day-to-day struggle to fulfill the Five-Year Plan, to raise the productivity of labor, to produce a maximum volume of consumer goods, of the finest quality, for the needs of the citizens of our Socialist country.

The peasants in the cooperatives, which they manage themselves, and the workers in the factories, which from now on they are going to manage themselves, are indeed today holding their future in their own hands.

VII

Address to the United Nations General Assembly

New York
September 22, 1960

Following herewith is the complete text of President Tito's address to the Fifteenth Session of the General Assembly of the United Nations, in which he makes a major exposition of Yugoslav foreign policy, with special attention to the problems of world peace, disarmament, and colonialism. This is Tito's most important address delivered outside Yugoslavia.

VII
United Nations Address

Mr. President: On behalf of the Yugoslav delegation, and in my own name, I wish to congratulate you on your election to the high and responsible post of the President of this important session of the General Assembly.

Mr. President, fellow delegates, may I be allowed to express my gratification at having the opportunity to attend the Fifteenth Session of the General Assembly here at United Nations headquarters. The peoples and the Government of Yugoslavia have always attached an exceptional significance to the United Nations as the broadest and most important international organization, whose basic objectives, particularly the maintenance of peace and security in the world, embody the fundamental aspirations and needs of the international community.

I also wish to express, on behalf of the Yugoslav delegation and in my own name, our satisfaction that the Fifteenth Session of the General Assembly is being attended by a large number of representatives of new members of the United Nations, particularly of the African countries that have only recently attained their independence. This increase in membership is of particular significance as it has, in a positive sense, made the structure of United Nations membership more complete; the basic aspirations of the new members of our organization are undoubtedly directed towards the consolidation of the independence they have achieved, towards a more rapid internal development, towards a status of equality in the community of nations, and towards a contribution of their own to the preservation of peace and to the stabilization of the world situation. Such aspirations are fully in accord with the spirit and letter of the Charter of the United Nations.

We hope that the United Nations will achieve real and complete universality in the near future through the attainment of independence by all the peoples now under colonial rule as well as through the recognition of the right of the People's Republic of China to be represented in the United Nations.

The Fifteenth Session of the General Assembly of the United Nations acquires special significance for more than one reason: above all because this Assembly is confronted with highly important and difficult tasks, and because it is taking place in an international atmosphere which causes grave concern, in an atmosphere marked by a revival of the cold war and by complete uncertainty as to where all this may lead in the future. In our opinion, the world has perhaps never at any time since the end of the war gone through such a period of uncertainty as it is going through today. It is for this very reason that we should all see to it that the activities of our organization and the manner in which they are carried out should always be in keeping with the spirit and the principles of the Charter and with the fundamental rights and sovereignty of each member state and of non-members as well. Otherwise, such activities would not serve their purpose and might well impair considerably the standing of the United Nations and the trust placed in the organization.

There is little difficulty, we believe, in tracing the causes of the present situation, a situation which, unless the utmost efforts are made within this international organization and already at the present session, might lead the world into a new catastrophe greater than any it has known in the past.

Fifteen years have elapsed since the end of World War II, and no solutions have yet been found to any of the major issues it left in its wake. I shall not attempt to describe here the course of events, but shall merely say what has already been said so many times, that the main reason why none of the major international questions has been solved is to be sought precisely in the fact that a wrong course was embarked upon from the very outset, a course which consisted in seeking to settle outstanding international issues from positions of strength, and one which is still persistently favored by certain influential circles.

What results has such a course brought to the world? It has led to a growing accumulation of new problems, which are straining more and more an already tense international atmosphere.

The world had placed considerable expectations in the summit meeting in Paris, and the failure of that conference caused profound disappointment, particularly in view of what had preceded its failure and had been one of the main causes of that failure. This has confirmed the conviction of peace-loving peoples that the fate of the world should not be left to the decisions of only a few states, no matter how big, but as the issues involved are of interest to all, they should be decided jointly by countries large and small, and primarily through the

United Nations and under its auspices, because it was precisely for this purpose that this international organization was established. That is why we attach such importance to this Fifteenth Session of the United Nations General Assembly.

We have not come here, of course, to heap more oil upon the fire or to side with any of the extreme attitudes that may reflect present tense international relations. We have come with a desire, above all, to contribute as much as possible to the easing of world tensions and to express our belief that the eleventh hour has struck to embark upon a new constructive course in international relations, upon a course of peaceful solutions of outstanding issues, a course of consolidation and of international cooperation based upon equality, as well as upon peaceful, active co-existence.

We do not delude ourselves that any final solution can be found here and now in the United Nations to the major issues that constitute a permanent threat to world peace. It would, however, we feel, be a major success if the view prevailed at this session that everything should be done to prevent a further deterioration of the international situation and an aggravation of the cold war atmosphere, that it is essential to secure such a composition and such activities of the United Nations bodies as to insure the performance of their functions in the most effective manner under the control of the organization. This has prompted us to work actively in favor of the idea that heads of states and of governments should attend this session personally in order not only to consolidate but to enhance still further the prestige attained by the United Nations.

The responsibility of us all is far greater than could have been visualized fifteen years ago when the United Nations came into being. In the course of these fifteen years we have, on the one hand, witnessed the unprecedentedly rapid and successful advance in the field of natural sciences and technology, and on the other, the increasingly vigorous, broad and active appearance on the stage of world history of the most numerous part of mankind that had hitherto been prevented from participating, on a footing of equality, in shaping its own destiny. However highly we may evaluate the positive contributions of the United Nations so far, we should not be blind to the fact that, under the stress of the political conflicts and dissensions of the post-war period, which were reflected within the organization, the latter has not been able to keep wholly abreast of the march of contemporary history.

There is a growing disparity between the brilliant successes achieved in the endeavor to harness the laws of nature to the service of man, and the deplorable conditions in which the majority of mankind lives, a mankind which still has to struggle for the elementary right to an existence worthy of man. Not only those peoples that still have to fight for their independence, often at the cost of heavy sacrifices in human lives, but also those that have already acceded to statehood still find themselves in practice in a position of inequality as against the highly developed countries.

The hopes that were aroused a year ago of a more substantial and more lasting easing of international tensions have, unfortunately, failed to materialize.

In contrast to last year's session, which took place in the atmosphere of Camp David, that is of East-West negotiations, this year we are meeting in the shadow of the failure of the summit conference, of the breaking off of the Geneva disarmament talks, and of the continual postponements in achieving the essential agreement on the banning of nuclear and thermonuclear weapons tests; in short, the tendency to increase tensions in East-West relations is growing and there is a revival of the cold war. These dangerous trends in the development of East-West relations are, on their part, creating an atmosphere of increasing mutual distrust.

These alarming trends have now also found expression in

the recent demand to equip the Bundeswehr with nuclear weapons, a demand which reveals the full gravity of the present international situation and would, if granted, diminish to a decisive degree the prospects of peace in Europe and in the world.

Although our people have, in the recent past, suffered severely at the hands of German militarism and Fascism, we harbor no feelings of hatred towards the German people. We are, however, deeply concerned by the revival of militarism in the Federal Republic of Germany. I feel I have, in this connection, to draw your particular attention to the mounting influence of military circles and to the revival of tendencies in Western Germany that ominously recall the past. Such tendencies can, however, only do harm to the genuine interests of the German people and increase tension and uncertainty in the world. On the other hand, those who foster or facilitate such tendencies, for the purpose of advancing their narrowly conceived interests, assume a heavy responsibility.

In this same period, owing to the policies pursued toward dependent and newly independent countries by the colonial powers, as well as by other powers that support this policy for various reasons, the war in Algeria continues endlessly, and conflicts and crises arise, as in the case of the Congo, of Cuba, Laos and West Irian, and seriously imperil world peace.

We cannot, as members of the United Nations, reconcile ourselves to such a state of affairs. Regardless of frequently differing views on this or that specific problem, or of a different appraisal of various situations and events, we can, all of us together, or at least a great majority of us, direct our efforts more energetically and more effectively towards a solution of the fundamental questions of our time.

We should not, in the first place, allow mistrust and tension to render impossible a constructive solution of the major issues upon which world peace depends. Foremost among these issues is the problem of disarmament, which has, in our era of technological progress, assumed an exceptionally serious significance.

However, amidst the conditions of a revival of the cold war, it is not the arms race alone which impedes the settlement of other fundamental issues. The unsolved problems of the colonial world and the problem of the attainment of genuine independence and economic progress by new and underdeveloped states also hamper the creation of the necessary international atmosphere for the initiation of disarmament and for cooperation in the spirit of peaceful co-existence.

The level of development reached by mankind and the crucial problems that have accompanied it increase our responsibility, but they augment, at the same time, our capabilities of impelling the course of history in a positive direction. It has frequently been said that the eyes of the world are turned towards this Assembly hall. Yet we must not forget that outside this hall there are hundreds of millions of people willing to support any constructive action on our part and to make it, through the power of their will and of their numbers, into a step forward towards peace and a better life for all nations, for the people of all continents.

II

Although the disarmament problem is the greatest among all the problems awaiting solution, I should nevertheless like first to turn my attention to the most acute colonial problem. This is particularly justified in view of the powerful upsurge of national liberation movements in Africa and elsewhere and, more especially, of recent events in the Congo, which do not concern that country alone, but also Africa as a whole and the further development of independent African peoples.

The process of the national, economic, political and cultural emancipation of former colonies is a historical necessity.

The liquidation of the obsolete economic, social and national relationships that constitute the essence of colonialism in its various forms makes it possible for numerous new states to emerge as constructive members of, and active factors in, the international community. These processes should not, therefore, be impeded; they should rather be approached in a constructive manner and the emergence of newly independent nations should be encouraged, since the ending of various forms of colonial relationships in the modern world is part of the efforts of the whole of mankind to achieve universal peace and progress.

Unfortunately, these processes are still meeting with a lack of understanding and with resistance. Many colonial powers and highly developed countries are unwilling to reconcile themselves to the ineluctable historical trends in Africa and in the other underdeveloped areas. They seek to block these processes in various larger or smaller areas, on the strength of their acquired positions and of their material and other advantages, or to alter their course by various political, economic and military means. Such efforts, doomed as they are by history, and futile in the final analysis, give rise to or aggravate conflicts and crises, such as the persistent continuation of the war in Algeria, the events in South Africa, the recent developments in the Congo, and, in a different context, the tension in Laos, or the situation relating to Cuba, where the people, under the leadership of their revolutionary government, won their freedom of which they had been deprived for so long, and are now exerting efforts to strengthen their independence on the basis of full equality. All these conflicts shake an already unstable world peace, the more so as they show an almost unavoidable tendency to become entangled with East-West antagonisms and conflicts. These cold war conflicts also threaten on their part to spread to areas which had been or are still under colonial domination, and to transform the newly independent countries into new hotbeds of strife and war dangers.

As an excuse for such outside interference, the alleged incapacity and immaturity of the newly liberated countries and their lack of economic development have been invoked, particularly of late. It cannot, however, possibly be a mere coincidence that, as a rule, the countries that had until recently not been free are also the least developed ones. Although it is a fact that the newly liberated countries encounter numerous difficulties in their development, it is also a fact that these difficulties stem primarily from a long period of colonial rule and that a continuation of colonial relationships could only multiply and increase them.

I feel I have, in this connection, to dwell in particular on the situation concerning the Republic of the Congo. The Congo has been the scene of the most typical manifestations of a negative colonial policy, of interference from without for the purpose of safeguarding the narrow interests of those forces and circles which cannot reconcile themselves to the loss of their privileged positions and interests.

The recognition of the independence of the Congo was construed by these circles merely as a façade behind which economic exploitation could be continued and other forms of dependence maintained. When this policy met with the resistance of the legitimate government of the Republic of the Congo, these circles resorted to various forms of more or less open interference, to the organizing of rebellion, to the secession of individual provinces, to the subversion of the government and so forth. Belgium, which had ruled the country and which persistently opposed the withdrawal of its troops, undoubtedly bears a particular responsibility for the adverse developments in the Congo. Part of the responsibility is shared by those who have supported or permitted such a course.

The intervention of the United Nations for the preservation

of peace was to have secured to the Congo development along such lines as would have safeguarded its independence, its sovereignty and territorial integrity, and as would have been in harmony with the interests of the people of the Congo and the rights of the lawful government. It is our profound belief, however, that the assistance of the United Nations has not proved to be sufficiently effective, primarily because there have been serious omissions and shortcomings in carrying out the resolutions of the Security Council.

The Government of the Federal People's Republic of Yugoslavia has repeatedly—including its request for the convening of the Security Council of 8 September 1960—set forth its views on the problem as a whole and has striven for what it considered to be a correct solution. We hope that appropriate ways and means will be found, on the basis, among other things, of the resolution recently adopted by the General Assembly at its emergency session, to protect and promote the strivings of the people of the Congo to maintain the independence and unity of their country. At the same time, it is essential that measures of necessary economic and technical assistance to the Congo be continued. The Yugoslav delegation will, for its part, support all measures in keeping with these aims.

The problem of the war in Algeria has been before us for five years now, but no progress towards a satisfactory solution has so far been made. The people of Algeria, who are continuing to make great sacrifices for the attainment of their freedom—thus placing all peoples fighting for peace, independence and equality in their debt—claim their natural and legitimate right to self-determination. This right was recognized by France, in principle, last year. Subsequent negotiations have unfortunately revealed that the French side has not drawn the practical conclusions deriving from the recognition of the right to self-determination. For this reason the conditions for negotiations were, naturally, unacceptable to the representatives of Algeria. Under these circumstances, the provisional government of Algeria is seeking a way out of the situation by means of a referendum under United Nations supervision, and we, for our part, can only welcome and support this proposal.

However, the continuation of the war in Algeria also has other, broader implications. If no early democratic solution is found, this will implicitly amount to a legalization of force as a means for suppressing the legitimate aspirations of a people and thus, in fact, a legalizing of war in general.

A specific and extremely dangerous aspect of these profoundly anti-historical tendencies, which are still at work on the African continent, is the ruthless policy of racial discrimination and oppression pursued by the Government of the Union of South Africa, a policy whose consequences have so tragically come to the fore this year. It is well-nigh incredible that it should be possible to conduct such a policy at the present time, in this latter half of the twentieth century, and in an area where liberation trends are so powerfully at work. This is certainly a problem to which the United Nations must devote an even greater—and more effective—attention than it has done hitherto.

If we probe more deeply into the problem of the liquidation of colonial relationships and analyze it in all its aspects, we shall easily come to the conclusion that the present tendency of the colonial powers to preserve, at all costs, their economic and other positions, even after the attainment of independence particularly by the African countries, is basically detrimental not only to the peoples which have achieved their independence, but also to the peoples of the colonial powers themselves. Such a policy cannot, in the long run, yield any benefits. It can only lead to new conflicts and do harm to both sides. Only relations based on equality between the peoples which have attained their independence and the peoples of the colonial powers can benefit both sides and can, moreover—and this is their most important feature—make such a policy into a powerful element in the safeguarding of peace and the promotion of constructive international cooperation. The implementation of such an approach to the question of relations between the newly liberated peoples and the peoples of the colonial powers would do away with the basic source of conflict and crisis, and remove the causes of antagonisms between countries in the backward and underdeveloped regions, on the one hand, and highly developed parts of the world, on the other.

The role of the United Nations in all these developments is of the highest significance both in the political and in the economic spheres. The United Nations should act effectively to insure that the processes of emancipation be speeded up and that they evolve with the least impediment; it should, at the same time, extend all-round and timely assistance to the countries which have set out along the road of independence so as to enable them to consolidate their independence and to give it the maximum substance. So far, the main concern of the United Nations in this respect has been to guide the trust territories towards independence as rapidly as possible and to speed up the evolution of other dependent territories towards independence. Thirty-five territories have achieved their freedom since the establishment of the United Nations, while several territories will attain their independence in the very near future. Twenty-nine formerly dependent territories have been admitted to the United Nations during the period under review. Now, however, our organization is faced with the tremendous task of providing this new freedom with full political and economic substance.

It is also quite obvious that the question of the final liquidation of colonial relationships is closely connected with the existence of the gap between the underdeveloped countries and the highly developed regions of the world, such as Europe and North America, and that it represents, moreover, one of the main causes of the continued existence and of the extension of this gap. It is from this and from backwardness in its most varied forms, it is from the economic weakness and dependence of certain countries and areas that conditions for interference from outside, for attempts to establish and redistribute "spheres of interest," necessarily arise. All this leads, as we are well aware, to political conflicts and hinders stabilization both in the political and in the economic fields.

In view of the experience so far, and of the fact that the granting of assistance and support is sometimes linked to political and economic conditions, while the granting of assistance on an individual basis is viewed by other states with the utmost suspicion and raises political problems, it is clear that to channel such assistance primarily through the United Nations is the best and most appropriate course. However, in view of the fact that the material resources of the United Nations are extremely limited due to the reluctance and refusal of wealthy states to place substantial means at the disposal of the United Nations for this purpose, it is clear that the newly liberated and underdeveloped countries cannot, under such conditions, rely solely upon assistance from the United Nations. One has to recognize their right to receive assistance from wherever they can obtain it, provided no political, economic or other conditions are attached.

The measures undertaken by the United Nations so far in this respect have undoubtedly been useful, but have been out of all proportion to the actual needs. If assistance through the United Nations were to continue on so limited a scale, at so slow a pace and in the manner in which it has been given so far, its effect could hardly be expected to tally with the interests of the consolidation of the countries concerned and of

world peace. We should then still be faced with the wholly unwarranted situation where the highly developed countries
spend on armaments a sum equal to the total production of
the underdeveloped countries, and where one-tenth of the production of our planet is being thrown into funds earmarked
for destruction and devastation instead of being directed towards the advancement and progress of mankind. One of the
most urgent tasks of the present session of the General Assembly is, therefore, to hasten, extend and render more effective
all forms of international assistance and of international
financing of the development of underdeveloped countries,
primarily through an increase of funds available to the United
Nations for the purpose. This, in fact, means that our organization should now undertake large-scale action for the purpose of providing broad and unselfish assistance to the newly
independent countries of Africa, so as to enable them to consolidate their independence and advance vigorously along the
path of economic, cultural and general progress.

The problem of the development of underdeveloped countries has assumed a particularly acute form in Africa, where
political and colonial relations are most persistently maintained and where they are intertwined with the consequences
of economic backwardness. The problems of Africa demand
the greatest efforts on our part. We consider as fully justified
the request that the United Nations take concerted action with
a view to technical, financial, and economic assistance to the
African continent. I am, therefore, in a position to state here
that my country is ready to consider, together with other
countries, the possibility of increasing assistance to the newly
liberated African countries in the form of experts, materials
and funds. My country is, at the same time, prepared to renounce a considerable part of the assistance it has hitherto been
receiving through the Technical Assistance Program of the
United Nations in favor of the new African countries.

The concentration of our efforts towards the solution of the problems of Africa should not, however, mean that we intend to neglect the problems of Latin America and Asia, with which we have been confronted for a decade now, and are even today confronted. A solution to the problems of Latin America is to be sought, in our view, primarily through an accelerated industrialization. The new economic conditions prevailing in the world call for a diversification of national economies. The awareness of the inevitability of this process should impel us to support and not seek to slow it down or impede it as this would be bound to provoke resistance and lead to political tension and conflicts, as shown particularly by the example of Cuba. In any case, we cannot consider as normal a situation where the markets of many Latin American products are placed at the mercy of the so-called free play of world "supply and demand." There is an obvious need for international action in this sphere.

Neither have the economic problems of Asia lost any of their urgency. The progress achieved by many Asian countries in the field of industrialization provides the best answer to the assertion advanced as recently as ten years ago to the effect that the underdeveloped countries did not have the natural resources and manpower required for industrialization in the modern sense. The Asian countries are successfully mastering the organizational problems of industrialization. They are making tremendous progress in the training of domestic industrial personnel. However, their efforts are greatly hampered by the lack of financial resources.

III

The next important and urgent problem I should like to examine is the question of disarmament.

The importance of disarmament, as one of the key problems of war and peace, is generally recognized. This awareness has not, however, in the attempts made hitherto to solve the problem, been translated into terms of essential practical measures. This has led to a situation where disarmament has assumed a specific role in international relations, a role whose significance is, it seems to me, even more crucial perhaps than has ever been the case before.

Therefore, we have to approach the solution of the problem of disarmament with a sense of extreme urgency. It should constantly be borne in mind that, as time passes, the armament race grows in intensity and that, as a result of this, each new measure of disarmament becomes more difficult and complicated. New and more dangerous types of weapons which are increasingly difficult to control, appear every day; the circle of countries possessing such armaments is expanding. Therefore, it is erroneous to speak, with regard to disarmament, of the continuation of the arms race; actually, this race is constantly gaining in speed, scope and intensity.

There are many ways of illustrating the absurd proportions assumed by the ever more intense armaments race as well as the extent of its negative consequences for mankind, but it is not my intention to do it here. The fact that the cost of a single B-70 super-bomber is equal to the total assistance extended through the United Nations for the development of underdeveloped countries in the course of one year points clearly to the urgent need of abandoning the course now being pursued.

As a concrete example, of a measure that we favor and which is essential to all, I shall mention the unwarranted delay in the reaching of an agreement for which all the objective preconditions have matured and which is demanded by public opinion throughout the world. I am referring to the prohibition of nuclear weapons tests. We believe that there are no longer any real obstacles in this respect, provided the great powers could reach a political understanding to conclude the negotiations, which have already lasted approximately two years, and come to an agreement, to which all countries should adhere.

This and any other genuine progress in the field of disarmament would have a favorable effect on international relations and would contribute considerably to their improvement. In the same way, any improvement in international relations, any progress in solving outstanding international issues—an aim towards which we should persistently strive—would have a favorable bearing on the solution of the disarmament problem. It follows, therefore, that the interdependence between the state of international relations and the situation in the field of disarmament is absolutely clear and direct. There is obviously no need to try to find out where to start, as it is obvious that the greatest efforts should be exerted in both directions.

It would be a mistake to believe that, in the unfolding of the process of international disarmament, everything would remain as it was before the cold war, the war preparations and the rest. The vicious circle would be broken and international relations would enter a new era. In fact, disarmament, if viewed in a sufficiently broad perspective, is a specific form of changing the world in a positive sense, as well as of relations therein. An ability to grasp this is, therefore, also required, as well as a readiness to place international relations upon a new basis.

This means that it is necessary, in order to make progress, to change certain established concepts and approaches, to abandon certain aims which obviously cannot be attained without war, to turn for the solution of international questions towards genuine peaceful co-existence among countries with different social systems.

The present so-called balance of armaments has reached so high and dangerous a level of military techniques and equipment that it is losing its *raison d'être* to an increasing degree every day. This balance does not insure security, as the protagonists of a certain policy want to make us believe. On the contrary, it is being transformed into a state of complete insecurity and presents a permanent mortal danger for mankind.

In order to create conditions in which the efforts for the attainment of disarmament might prove successful, it is obviously essential—as I have already said—to create a minimum of favorable atmosphere and an indispensable degree of mutual confidence. Unfortunately, an opposite course has too often been followed in the past.

For instance, it cannot be assumed that it is possible, at one and the same time, successfully to negotiate and to violate the sovereignty and national frontiers of the negotiating partners regardless of the motives invoked for justifying such harmful practices.

Similarly, as an expression of the negative views of those who are unable—even in the present condition marked by the existence of missiles and nuclear weapons—to renounce the potential use of force and war as a means of solving international disputes, we also come across various theories on the possibility, or even harmlessness, of local wars. These theories are put forward despite a number of extremely eloquent experiences derived in this respect from the post-war period, although precisely the opposite should have become clear to everybody, namely, that any local war inevitably tends, under present world conditions, to turn into a general war. The trend towards so-called tactical nuclear weapons is bound to have the same effect.

What is the only lasting positive alternative to the present negative developments in this sphere? We are firmly convinced that the realization of general and complete disarmament alone provides such an alternative. This is precisely the reason why the Yugoslav Government has—in addition to the support given to other comprehensive measures leading towards general and complete disarmament—welcomed the proposal set forth in the statement of the Prime Minister of the Union of Soviet Socialist Republics, Mr. Khrushchev, to the General Assembly of the United Nations on 18 September 1959, as well as later Soviet proposals indicating a broad and direct approach to actual disarmament measures.

We are firmly convinced that general and complete disarmament is not an unrealistic aim, but rather the only possible and lasting solution. It is sufficiently well known, I believe, that the Yugoslav Government has always worked comprehensively and actively in the United Nations and elsewhere towards a solution of the problem of disarmament.

The problems of balance and control have often been placed in the forefront of negotiations so far. Provided there is a readiness and a sincere willingness to advance towards genuine disarmament, these problems should not, we feel, be allowed to become intractable and to constitute an obstacle to an agreement because, intrinsically, they are not and should not constitute such an obstacle. The question of balance should, of course, be taken into account in the concrete process of disarmament, as it would be unrealistic to expect any country to accept a proposal which might, at a given moment, or in a given period, place it in a position of obvious inferiority. It would be, however, extremely harmful to seek to establish an abstract and absolute balance in advance, as no such balance exists in the process of armament either.

The same applies to the control of disarmament. It is not possible to question, nor does anyone actually question, the need for adequate, strict control as a function of disarmament. On the other hand, to insist upon the introduction of far-reaching measures of control before undertaking measures of actual disarmament is only another way of opposing disarmament. Satisfactory compromises regarding the control problem are possible, if control is viewed within the context of solving the problem of disarmament and of the achievement of certain practical measures within a given process.

While giving its support to general and complete disarmament, and thus to the proposals made to this effect, the Yugoslav Government would be prepared to accept certain measures as part of the process leading to general and complete disarmament; such measures would, by their very nature, stimulate both further agreements and the solutions of the problem of disarmament in its entirety. What we have in mind here are genuine measures of a radical nature, with a visible and direct material and political effect, measures apt to contribute towards advancing the technological process essential to disarmament (what I have in mind is the development and application of control, etc.). The discontinuance of nuclear tests provides the best example of such a measure. Similar useful measures could, in the light of the above conditions, be the following: the reduction of military expenditure and the utilization of the savings effected in this way, or of part of these savings, for assistance to underdeveloped countries; the transfer of fissionable materials for peaceful uses, as well as disengagement in Central Europe. Taken together, these measures should provide a pattern of advance at the beginning and within the framework of essential progress towards general disarmament. The best thing would be, of course, to achieve the most substantial results as soon as possible; it seems to me, however, that the steps I have outlined are significant enough to lead rapidly to major results.

The Fifteenth Session of the General Assembly is undoubtedly called upon, even more so than had been the case in the past, to help establish an appropriate procedure and machinery for disarmament negotiations.

A more appropriate procedure than the one applied so far would certainly make it possible for developments in the field of disarmament finally to take a more favorable turn. The forms used in the past have obviously not proved very fortunate. The frameworks which had been laid down were either too narrow and one-sided, or too broad and rigid, for the conduct of practical negotiations.

It is a fact that the great powers have a particular responsibility with regard to the question of disarmament, and thus also specific obligations towards the world. For this reason we have, for a number of years, through the establishment of the Five-Power Sub-Committee and later through the setting up of the Ten Nation Committee on Disarmament, entrusted the great powers with the task of finding a basis for agreement on disarmament and of evolving methods for the realization of such an agreement. It is well known that no results have been achieved; the negotiations were interrupted and the problem of disarmament has again been placed before the United Nations at the initiative of the great powers themselves.

It would therefore be necessary, for the purpose of conducting disarmament negotiations, to find a solution along the lines of a negotiating body which would be more effective and constituted on a broader basis than the Ten Nation Committee on Disarmament. The composition of the negotiating body should be such as to reflect more adequately the political structure of the present-day world and the principle of geographic representation. This would also insure a more stable equilibrium in the negotiating body which might help avoid the difficulties soon encountered by the Ten Nation Committee based on the concept of mechanical equilibrium between the representatives of the two military alignments. On the other hand, the negotiating body should evidently be better suited to the performance of the operative tasks of negotiating than has been the case with the United Nations Disarmament Commission, which—I wish to lay particular emphasis on this—has a positive place and, perhaps, a lasting importance as an expression of the common interest and responsibilities of the entire membership of the United Nations in regard to the disarmament problem. An appropriate and acceptable machinery could perhaps be found within the general framework of the commission.

Efforts should be made in this respect to make proper use of the time and work of the present session of the Assembly in order to reach at least a basic agreement on the renewal of the negotiations on disarmament. The whole world awaits this on our part. The Yugoslav delegation will, for its part, participate with the greatest interest, in the course of this session, in the consideration of various aspects of the disarmament problem as well as in the possible study of new proposals, striving, as it has done in the past, to appraise objectively and to support all the elements that can bring us closer to a solution.

IV

If the modern world is to cope successfully with the problems I have just mentioned as well as with all the other problems upon which peace and the future of mankind depend, it is indispensable that all peoples, without exception, should accept the principles of co-existence and, what is more, apply them in their mutual relations everywhere and on every occasion.

In our opinion, the essence of peaceful and active co-existence should contain important elements that are not yet generally accepted in international relations, a fact which poisons in various ways and to a growing extent the relations between peoples and states in the world.

The first fundamental principle of co-existence, as we understand it, is that different social systems must not be a reason for war conflicts or stand in the way of peaceful cooperation among states and peoples.

The second fundamental principle of peaceful co-existence is that various controversial issues should be settled in a peaceful way, and that force and war should be eliminated from the practice of international relations.

The third fundamental principle is the observance of the obligation of non-interference in the internal affairs of other peoples and states and the right of every people to organize its own internal development and its own life.

Peaceful and active co-existence is now gaining momentum in the world in the technical, cultural and even, to a certain extent, in the political fields with regard to relations among states with different social systems. Why should artificial obstacles be placed in the way of this, the only correct process of development in the world? Why should misinformation, falsehood and even hatred among peoples be disseminated through the press, in speeches and in other ways? Why should antiquated, obsolete methods and procedures persistently be used in the modern world where they are not only anachronistic but also pose a constant threat to the peace and progress of mankind? These are precisely the elements that impede the proper development of international relations and cooperation. It is, of course, completely illusory to expect that peace will prevail among nations, that they will be able to face the future without fear, if this world of ours continues to be a world where there is no equality between big and small states and nations, where those that have more consider it to their advantage that others have been left behind, or where it is believed that the arms race and the continuation of the cold war are the best means of national policy, and that the policy of force and strength is the surest way towards the fulfillment of their aspirations, whether justified or unjustified, and to solve outstanding problems.

Co-existence among nations therefore imposes itself not only as a practical necessity but also as an imperative in the present conditions. There is no alternative to this except to live in a state of almost constant "cold war," or to walk along

"the verge of war," and finally to have a real war, which
would mean complete destruction, and this we must all dis-
card.

It is for this reason that it is no longer sufficient to define
war as a "continuation of policy by other means." The orientation towards war for the solving of international disputes
has become a component of a policy which is no longer capable of convincing otherwise than by threats or use of force.
The fundamental principles of co-existence are really a living
and creative interpretation of the spirit and principles of the
Charter of our organization. By acceding to membership, we
pledge ourselves to observe and apply these principles, and
thus also to pursue an international policy fully in harmony
with the concepts and practice of co-existence among nations,
regardless of their racial, ideological or other differences.
That is why it is completely incompatible with the principles
of co-existence, and consequently with the principles of the
United Nations Charter, not merely to preach and apply a
policy of force and of the right of the stronger, but also to
preach and apply racial discrimination, to interfere in the internal affairs of others under ideological and political pretexts,
to exert economic pressure and discrimination of the stronger
against the weaker; to apply any method of moral and political pressure.

On the other hand, no less erroneous is the notion that co-
existence should mean the preservation of existing relations, as
in areas under colonial rule for instance, and in other regions
where the stronger and the more developed have built up privileged positions in weaker and underdeveloped countries. Such
a notion is in flagrant contradiction to the spirit and significance of co-existence, which cannot serve to halt historical
processes in international life. On the contrary, it stimulates
and facilitates these processes without endangering world
peace, but rather makes it more stable. Because our views on

the concept of co-existence are such, we cannot accept the view that in the present world co-existence should be confined to insuring the co-existing of the existing groupings. Of course, co-existence between them should also be sought in order to replace present tensions and mistrust, but not with the intention of stopping at such co-existence, but rather of making it a starting point towards more active relations and more fruitful and broader cooperation among all states and nations including those that today hold antagonistic positions. Bearing all this in mind, we consider that the true observance of the principles of co-existence is proved and tested only through actual practice, that is, above all through the extent to which a given policy, and given political concepts and actions contribute to the strengthening of peace.

The country on behalf of which I am speaking here today, the Federal People's Republic of Yugoslavia, has, ever since its birth, sought to establish relations with countries from various parts of the world on such a basis. Owing to this, we believe that our country has contributed not only to its own national interests and aspirations, but also to the general cause of the world. As a fully independent country, it acts in the conviction that it follows a course which, in the present world, leads most surely to peace and to active international cooperation. Pursuing such a course, my country has established fruitful relations with all the nations that were ready to cooperate on the basis of mutual respect, equality and non-interference. On the other hand, Yugoslavia has met along this road a number of countries and peoples from all continents which, guided by the same aspirations, constituted a beneficial force of peace in the days of the cold war. In the present changed international conditions these countries and peoples have proved to be the most consistent protagonists of efforts for the realization of co-existence in the world, for peace based on progress and equal rights. These independent countries have therefore turned, in the first place, towards our organization, seeing in it and its Charter a powerful instrument for the realization of their own aspirations, as well as the general strivings of mankind. It is up to us to prove at the present session of the Assembly, by the decisions which we are going to take, more than we have done before, that their trust in our organization has been justified.

I believe that the Assembly should, at its present session, adopt certain general directives perhaps in the form of a declaration by the General Assembly relating to the efforts and rules of conduct which are essential in order to eliminate international tension, to promote peaceful and good-neighborly relations among states and to develop international cooperation in all spheres.

All of us here, representatives of countries large and small alike, are faced with the momentous and unique task to make it possible, through our common efforts, for the peoples and nations of the world to advance towards a more radiant future.

I have set forth here our views concerning certain international problems that we consider to be of the greatest importance and urgency today. In defining our attitudes on various questions, we always endeavor to be guided by certain principles, which constitute the foundation of our entire foreign policy; these principles, as I have already said, are merely a cementation of the principles embodied in the Charter of the United Nations.

May I, in conclusion, summarize our views.

We believe and maintain that there is no other alternative to active, peaceful co-existence in the world of today and tomorrow. By this we mean the possibility and necessity of developing lasting cooperation among countries with different social and political systems.

With regard to the crucial question of disarmament, we are

faced by a seemingly insoluble contradiction. On the one hand, war is becoming ever more absurd owing to the appalling destructive capabilities of contemporary weapons. On the other hand, the piling up of ever more destructive weapons itself leads to war. It is evident that only a prevention of the further accumulation of weapons—that is, disarmament—can provide a solution. In this sense we insist that disarmament talks should be renewed as soon as possible within an adequate framework. If no agreement on general disarmament can be reached at the present moment, we should be ready to engage in a partial agreement. Once the idea of a partial agreement is accepted, we must be ready to face the fact that such an agreement will fall short of perfection. The risks involved are obviously incomparably smaller than those contained in the present completely uncontrolled armaments race.

This point of view of ours also determines our attitude to certain tendencies that may lead to a general division of the world and which evidently constitute one of the basic negative facts and elements of contemporary international life and one of the main causes of the so-called cold war. Therefore, any extension and aggravation of this struggle necessarily leads to the intensification of the cold war, to propaganda moves, to extreme and exclusive attitudes, and to the alignment of all countries according to these attitudes—thus further deforming and straining international relations, intensifying and aggravating existing disputes, provoking new conflicts and rendering agreement more difficult.

We have always endeavored, especially in tense situations, to take a stand on various proposals and initiatives not according to the side from which they come, but in terms of their significance for the strengthening of peace.

We have thus given full support to the Soviet proposal on general and complete disarmament and do so today. We shall continue to act in this way in the future and lend our support to any initiative, regardless where it comes from, which, in our opinion, contributes to the strengthening of peace.

It follows from all that I have said, that we do not see a way out of the very dangerous situation in which the world finds itself in alignment with one side or the other, still less in an aggravation of the struggle between them. We believe that a way out can be found in a gradual overcoming of the obstacles that this struggle brings in its wake and in the gradual superseding and eliminating of the existing military alliances. It is, namely, evident that co-existence in the atmosphere of the arms race can in no way provide a basis for a lasting and stable peace. On the contrary, peace can be insured and strengthened only through the development of broad cooperation on all questions of general interest and through a resolute struggle for disarmament and for the abolition of unequal relations.

Finally, we believe and maintain that war is no longer inevitable, or rather that there exist real prospects for its permanent elimination as an instrument of policy and means of settling international disputes. Our conviction is based on an estimate that those forces in the world which incline towards war for the attainment of their objectives, and which are accordingly preparing for war, can be isolated and rendered harmless by the consistent policy of peace. In other words, we believe that the overwhelming majority of mankind is opposed to war, that the material and social and political conditions for the maintenance of peace are maturing increasingly, and that the forces in the world which are against war are today sufficiently strong and capable of preventing its outbreak.

These are the basic principles by which Yugoslav foreign policy is guided. I think that the explanation I have given will contribute towards a better understanding of both these principles and of our entire foreign policy. I am convinced that within this framework it will be clear why and in what sense we are attaching particular importance to the contribution that the so-called non-committed countries can make towards the betterment of international relations and as to the great role that the United Nations can and should play in this respect.

VIII

Address to the Belgrade Conference of Nonaligned Countries

Belgrade
September 3, 1961

Following herewith is the complete text of President Tito's address to the Belgrade Conference of Heads of State or Government of Nonaligned Countries. In this address before the representatives of twenty-nine nations, including an emperor, two kings, nine presidents, and five prime ministers, President Tito expounds the goals and aspirations of the nonaligned, developing nations of the "Third World."

VIII
Nonaligned Countries

M r. Chairman, dear friends: May I, first of all, thank you on behalf of the government and peoples of Yugoslavia for the very cordial and friendly words addressed to our people and government, as well as to me personally, in your speeches. I wish to stress once again that our people are greatly honored to have the opportunity to extend their hospitality to such a large number of distinguished guests who have come to our country on such a noble mission.

Mr. Chairman, I would like to deal in this statement with the most important problems which are causing so much concern to mankind at present and each of which, taken separately, constitutes a threat to world peace. These problems have actually impelled us to convene this meeting of the highest representatives of nonaligned countries.

Perhaps we were wrong to labor for too long a time under the delusion that the most responsible statesmen of the great powers would find a way towards the peaceful solution of the problems of which I am going to speak. It was perhaps no less mistaken to believe that small countries, and the nonaligned countries in particular, are not qualified to exert greater efforts for the solution of international problems and to voice more resolutely their views with regard to these problems and that this should be the concern of the great powers alone. There is no doubt, however, that the current situation is too serious and dangerous to allow such a state of affairs to continue. Now it is necessary to concentrate all the efforts and forces moving for peace in the world, in order to contribute to the victory of peace through more resolute action. In their peaceful policies the representatives of nonaligned countries can rely not only upon the peoples of their own countries but also upon peace-loving forces throughout the world, including the peoples of countries belonging to blocs.

We shall be happy if we succeed in contributing, through our objective evaluation of the existing situation in international relations and through our constructive proposals, to the improvement of the international situation. Proceeding from this, I shall dwell in my statement mainly on the five most important questions, which are engaging today, to an ever greater extent, the attention not only of leading statesmen in the world but also of all the peoples in general. These problems are: general disarmament, the present crisis regarding Berlin, colonialism, economic problems and assistance to less developed countries, and what we call active and peaceful coexistence.

I

First of all, I wish to refer to the question of disarmament. Since the time when the Premier of the Soviet Union, Nikita

Sergeyevich Khrushchev, submitted a proposal on general disarmament to the United Nations, this question has not, in effect, moved a step further. We are witnessing an incomprehensible game with this really key problem; a key problem both because it constitutes a constant threat to peace and because it is draining enormous material resources which could be used for promoting the well-being and prosperity not only of the peoples of those countries which possess and spend these resources, but of all peoples in general. Everyone pays lip service to disarmament. However, in actual practice, when it is a question of practical solutions, obstacles are raised and counter-proposals made, which actually prevent any agreement from being reached.

For a long time there was a question as to what should be given priority: inspection or disarmament? However, in order to control something, a process which needs to be controlled should evolve, that is to say, a process of genuine disarmament. And in order that this process may evolve, it is necessary to reach, first of all, in principle and concretely, an agreement on general disarmament. This is a logic which cannot be refuted. To oppose such a logic, means to indulge in mere propaganda and no sober-minded person can be convinced that this propaganda is sincere. Now, from the formal point of view, matters stand somewhat differently. The formula on general and complete disarmament, accompanied by strict international control, has been generally accepted. However, in reality, up till now nothing has changed, nothing has turned for the better. It is true that talks are continuing, but they have been going on without any success for years, and for the time being there is still no sign that any effective rapprochement of views has taken place. In the meantime, the arms race is continuing and assuming ever greater proportions, accompanied by the production and piling up of increasing quantities of ever more destructive weapons of mass annihilation.

In outlining our position on the question of disarmament, I have not lost sight of the fact that general and complete disarmament is not an unrealistic aim, but is, on the contrary, the only possible lasting solution, which must be attained in order to enable mankind to embark upon a new road towards the establishment of better relations among nations.

In order to inaugurate the process leading to the solution of the problem of disarmament, it is obvious that not only more intense efforts, but a new approach to this problem are today called for. This new approach calls for the broad and active participation also of those countries which have neither been involved in the arms race nor directly engaged in disarmament negotiations. Here I am thinking of those countries in particular whose approach to this problem, in view of their role in international affairs, is not burdened with the thought of safeguarding their own interests and prestige and which are able, therefore, to discern more objectively the possibilities for the solution of the disarmament question and are ready to strive to the utmost towards that end.

Perhaps the time has come to consider the possibility of convening a general world disarmament conference, as a means for moving this problem off dead center. This, of course, does not mean diminishing the role of the great nuclear powers in a field where they will continue to bear the main responsibility. This should merely result in the creation of conditions where these powers also could and, in a sense, would have to adjust their positions to the genuine requirement of settling the disarmament problem.

Of course, when speaking of a new approach, what I have in mind is not that we should seek a kind of illusory middle course between the opposing positions of one and the other side, but that we should proceed in the sense of objective requirements and an effective advance in the field of disarmament. Twelve Asian and African countries and Yugoslavia—

all of which are present at this conference—submitted a resolution to the Fifteenth Session of the General Assembly of the United Nations, embodying the essential elements of a positive platform for further efforts towards disarmament.

In principle, all are actually in agreement that general and complete disarmament may be achieved through specific stages, none of which should upset the balance of power to the detriment of one state or group of states. Here, as well as in the case of other aspects of the disarmament problem, the difficulties encountered do not derive primarily from the nature of things (although, of course, there are such difficulties also), but to a larger extent from what I have just mentioned, namely from a stubborn tendency to view the very process of disarmament, too, insofar as it ought to take place, as a means for gaining military ascendancy.

No one denies the need of strict international control, although such control is still presented by some—and, in fact, frequently taken advantage of—as an obstacle to an agreement on disarmament. Viewed as part of the actual disarmament process, the problem of inspection, as a means of insuring that the various agreed disarmament measures are carried out, is not of such a nature as to render an appropriate solution unduly difficult. Therefore, the tendency of those who continue to make a "fetish" out of control cannot be viewed otherwise than as an indication of their unwillingness or hesitation to undertake real disarmament.

In the present state of profound crisis in the field of disarmament, it appears to me that special importance should be attached to the question of initial and partial measures. These measures, of course, should not be construed as an alternative to complete disarmament, which remains the basic and increasingly urgent task. These measures, however, provided they are really aimed at genuine disarmament, could create more favorable conditions for initiating the process of disarmament and could even contribute directly towards this process.

I believe, for example, that the first in a series of such measures could be the decision of all countries to reduce their military expenditures, coupled with an obligation to contribute and utilize part of the savings thus achieved for assistance to economically less developed countries, as this would provide at least some guarantee that such a reduction has taken place. If this could not be done immediately, then, perhaps, a decision to freeze military budgets at their January 1, 1960, levels could be taken.

In my speech at the Fifteenth Session of the General Assembly of the United Nations, if I may recall it, I specifically mentioned, as some of the possible initial and partial measures in the field of disarmament, such a reduction of military expenditures as well as the transfer of fissionable materials for peaceful uses and measures of disengagement in Central Europe and elsewhere. In my mind, all these measures are still of considerable urgency.

Is it realistic and possible to speak seriously of disarmament when, at the same time, expenditures on armaments and the production of the most modern means of destruction are being tremendously increased? There is no logic here, but an obvious discrepancy between words and deeds. This proves that those who endeavor, and while they endeavor, to solve outstanding issues from a position of strength cannot exert genuine efforts towards disarmament. If one sincerely wishes to undertake disarmament, it is first of all necessary, at least, to call a halt to further armaments!

The negotiations on the discontinuance of nuclear weapons tests have also reached an impasse. What is even worse, a Western power which is a member of the Atlantic Pact—France —has failed to comply with the resolutions of the United Nations on the discontinuance of atomic tests, but continues to carry out such tests, while the other Western powers possessing atomic armaments have not taken any resolute measures against this. The matters have now reached a point where the Soviet Government has published a statement on the resumption of nuclear weapons tests. We are not surprised so much by the communiqué on the resumption of atomic and hydrogen weapons tests, because we could understand the reasons adduced by the government of the USSR. We are surprised more by the fact that this was done on the day of the opening of this conference of peace. All this has alarmed the whole world to an even greater extent. We consider that utmost efforts should be exerted in order to bring about a resumption of negotiations on this problem. It should be examined in all seriousness and in a constructive spirit, because the present moment is decisive for the taking of urgent measures in order to prevent the worst.

It is, of course, extremely important that a final stop should be put to nuclear weapons tests, as they, too, endanger human life. But it is just as necessary to destroy the accumulated stockpiles of nuclear arms, as they are liable to destroy the whole world—and every man on earth stands in great fear precisely of these weapons. This can be done more easily today than tomorrow, when many other countries will have such means at their disposal and when inspection will become almost impossible. Do we not, therefore, run the risk that an irresponsible lunatic, a modern Herostratos, or, what is even worse, a Hitler, might endanger the whole of mankind?

I consider the solution of the disarmament question to be a matter of the greatest urgency and I believe that all of us in this hall are in agreement on this, because a constructive approach to this problem becomes increasingly difficult with the passing of time, particularly because of the attitude of the great powers. The world which sees in this a real danger for itself, must speak up resolutely and this is precisely what we are here for.

II

Mr. Chairman, The question of Germany and the recent deterioration of the Berlin situation are also in the center of world attention today.

Can we remain passive observers in the face of an international atmosphere which is, in this connection, approaching the point of explosion?

The Berlin dispute, which has now been revived, has ominous overtones, while a solution of the German problem has already been delayed sixteen years. The existence of two Germanys is an actual fact today that cannot be denied, as it is the legacy of the war and of sixteen years of post-war development. Great changes have occurred on both sides: in Eastern Germany, the entire social development has followed a Socialist course, which has assumed, during the period of sixteen years of development, an ever more pronounced new social character in all spheres of social life. On the other hand, Western Germany has been restored; it has a typically capitalist social system, fraught and interwoven with remnants of Fascist and revanchist conceptions and tendencies, which give cause for grave concern.

Who can guarantee that this danger will not assume again, tomorrow, proportions liable to inflict new miseries upon mankind? Tens of millions of victims of Fascist insanity demand that a different course should be taken in order to prevent similar tragedies in the future. This must be the path of the democratization, and not of the militarization, of Germany. Thus only can a sound basis for a correct and lasting solution of the German problem be established, and in this respect it is the German people who will have to say the last word concerning their own future.

Had a policy aimed at the democratization and not militarization of Western Germany been initiated and pursued in a consistent manner immediately after the Second World War, a quieter situation would prevail today and the problem of Germany would have been perhaps already solved. As it is, we are again on the verge of a situation fraught with the danger of war. And why? First and foremost, because of the shortsighted and incomprehensible policies pursued by some powers who, I do not know why, believe that an armed and militaristic Germany will represent a factor of security in Europe. However, the ever more intensive arming of Western Germany is bound to result in an ever greater strengthening of those reactionary and Fascist elements which have been left behind by Hitler's war machine and which had carried out Hitler's orders not only at the various fronts, but also in the rear, where they endeavored to annihilate whole nations.

We all know that the situation regarding Berlin has recently become much worse. There is even talk of an armed conflict, if the Soviet Union signs a peace treaty with Eastern Germany and transfers to the latter the sovereign rights of control over the approaches to West Berlin, etc. Is it really possible that the idea of going to war because of this should have occurred to some people, that the world should be thrown into a new catastrophe because of this? Whoever started anything of the kind would have the entire peace-loving public opinion of the world against him. I consider that it is necessary to talk and to negotiate on this question in order to find at least a provisional solution, which would not prejudge a final settlement to be achieved later. When I say later, I do not mean that this question should be preserved in order to be resurrected at the first opportunity as a hotbed of new conflict, but that it is necessary to find a reasonable way out of this situation with a view to overcoming the existing tension, which, in addition to threatening peace, makes it impossible to set about the settlement of other major issues and to create favorable conditions for their final solution.

The road leading to a settlement of the German problem —and I wish to emphasize at this point that I do not have in mind the already settled question of the Oder-Neisse border —is not one consisting in arming one or the other side and in further aggravating relations between the Federal Republic of Germany and the German Democratic Republic, but gradually exploring ways and means for the peaceful and constructive cooperation between the two German states and at promoting all that brings them together. The solution of the present Berlin crisis, which is the result of an abnormal situation, should be sought solely in negotiations and in the elimination of those elements which are causing this question to be a potential and dangerous source of a new conflict.

III

Dear friends, I believe that we all agree that the colonial problem, which is of special interest to the participants in the conference, is one of the major outstanding problems. It is, at the same time, a world problem and it can be said that it plays an almost decisive role within a complex of problems that make the present situation in the world so extremely tense and complicated.

It is simply unbelievable how some colonial powers cannot, or do not want, to understand the spirit of our times and the processes which are now taking place. They cannot resign themselves to the ineluctable historical process which is now taking place in Africa and Asia; they cannot resign themselves to the fact that the last hour of colonialism has struck. In this they do not hesitate to resort to the most savage bloodshed and terror against unarmed peoples, nor do they hesitate to apply economic pressure and other methods in order to prolong, somehow or other, their colonial, imperialist rule, under any form and at any price, even at the cost of provoking armed conflicts fraught with unforeseeable consequences. This is also clearly demonstrated by the recent French armed attack against and the bombing and machine-gunning of the innocent inhabitants of Bizerta, in Tunisia. This incident can also serve as a lesson that—due to the fact that the colonial question has not yet been fully settled and in the absence of firm guarantees by the United Nations—the attainment of full independence by colonial peoples becomes highly problematic.

The acts of savagery committed by the Portuguese armed forces against the barehanded populations of Angola are causing indignation throughout the world. Tens of thousands of men, women and children have already been killed. These developments are viewed, however, calmly both by the Portuguese colonialists and, unfortunately, by those powers which have, for their own reasons, adopted a benevolent attitude towards the latter, assuming thereby a share of the grave responsibility. However, millions of men, not only in Africa and Asia, but in the whole world, cannot remain indifferent to these events. Every form of assistance should be extended to the people of Angola in their struggle for independence. We must resolutely demand, not only here but especially in the United Nations, that Angola be granted full independence in the shortest period of time. The centuries-old slavery must be terminated as soon as possible. Otherwise, this age-long disgrace will be borne by the generations of the twentieth century.

We find the same or a similar case in South Africa. Racial discrimination in the Union of South Africa is a dishonor to the civilized world. The treatment of the autochthonous populations by South Africa's colonialist rulers constitutes a brutal offence against human dignity and humane principles. The cynical and brutal rejection and mockery of those principles is arousing a mounting wave of indignation throughout the world. We cannot, however, confine ourselves to expressions of indignation and protest, but must take more effective and concerted action, such as will compel the protagonists of this unheard-of arbitrary rule to bow to the decisions of the United Nations. The various resolutions adopted by the United Nations as well as actions taken pursuant to these resolutions have proved ineffective so far. It seems as if the rulers of that country were treating the decisions taken so far with scorn. What does this mean? It means that more severe sanctions should be applied.

In the course of the seven-year-old heroic struggle of the Algerian people, streams of the blood not only of the fighters at the front but also of the peaceful civilian population have been shed. What an absurd situation has been created as a result of the attempts to hang on, at any cost, to something that was conquered by force several decades ago! Rarely has a people paid such a high price for its right to be master in its own country. It is simply inconceivable what a stubborn resistance the colonialists are putting up in that unfortunate country against something that is historically ineluctable. The forces opposing colonialism have grown to huge proportions today. The more blood is shed, the wider will be the gulf between the peoples of Algeria and France. We are all awaiting impatiently that common sense should prevail and that an agreement should be reached at the negotiations between the representatives of the provisional government of the Republic of Algeria and the representatives of France, an agreement which will finally recognize the right of the Algerian people to freedom and independence. Not only will the people of Algeria be free then, but the people of France will also be freed from a great stain of dishonor.

Permit me to refer briefly to the present situation in the Congo. In my opinion, the situation is still not clear; surprises are still possible, unless the organs of the United Nations show the utmost vigilance and energy in the prevention of any outside interference, unless they insure the regular and unimpeded functioning of the parliament, and the new government. We saw that the monstrous murder of the Prime Minister of the legitimate Congolese Government, Patrice Lumumba, and of other Congolese leaders could not shake the people of the Congo in its determination to fight against the colonialists and domestic mercenaries. This murder only served to intensify the resistance of the people who have succeeded in setting in motion a certain process leading towards the easing of the situation in that country. It would be an unforgivable error, if we failed to draw a lesson from this recent tragedy, and if we failed to do all within our power to prevent it from occurring again and to help the national forces of the Congo in the consolidation of their internal conditions and in the strengthening of the unity and integrity of the country.

The best evidence of the confusion that can be caused by outside interference is provided by the case of Laos, where the situation is not clear even today. Laos is again threatened with civil war, which, in turn, owing to interference from outside, might become the dangerous hotbed of an armed conflict of wider proportions and far-reaching consequences.

As far as West Irian is concerned, it is really high time for the colonialists in distant Europe, who are in possesion of that colony, to realize how senseless it is to oppose the liberation of West Irian from colonial bondage and its union with Indonesia—its mother country. The people of Indonesia will, of course, never renounce its right to that part of its country and it would be, therefore, better if this question was settled in a peaceful manner as promptly as possible.

The best illustration of how deeply ingrained are the aspirations of the peoples to liberate themselves from all elements of colonial and semi-colonial dependence is provided by the recent attempt at aggressive intervention in Cuba, where the whole people unanimously rose in arms to oppose it. That could, and should, also serve as a lesson that nations do not wish to suffer outside interference in the life of their country.

I have mentioned here some of the most important colonial problems, each of which in itself constitutes a danger to world peace. But there are also quite a number of colonial peoples, whose liberation and independence are an essential prerequisite for the removal of one of the major causes of the present tension in the world and constant danger of the outbreak of armed conflicts.

The process of emancipation from colonialism is particularly hampered by the fact that the cold war is being transposed into the colonial regions.

The elimination of colonial relationships and of neo-colonialistic attempts at preserving the substance of colonialism in changed circumstances is today equally to the advantage of colonial peoples and of the peoples of metropolitan countries. Full support to peoples and countries struggling against colonial domination for their fundamental rights is, at the same time, one of the basic prerequisites for an effective eradication of sources of war and of dangers threatening world peace.

Responding to the demands of colonial peoples and of the peoples of the world in general, and stressing the need to insure progress in the contemporary world, the General Assembly of the United Nations adopted at its Fifteenth Session, in 1960, the "Declaration on the Granting of Independence to Colonial Countries and Peoples." The declaration provides the most adequate legal and political basis, on which it is today both necessary and possible to carry out the abolition of colonial relationships in all their forms, in full harmony with the interests of the maintenance and strengthening of peace among nations.

What still remains to be done after this historic decision—

which constitutes a unique contribution of independent policy and of the United Nations to the cause of world progress and peace—is to adopt provisions providing for the requisite measures and for early, precisely defined target dates for the implementation of the anti-colonial declaration; this ought to be done in a manner which will provide ample assurance that the peoples in the colonies will take over the government of their own countries, namely, that they will attain genuine independence and true national freedom.

IV

There is no doubt that the final eradication of colonialism depends also to a large extent on the elimination of differences between the economically less developed and highly developed regions in the world. These differences are today the source of numerous conflicts, of many attempts at interfering in and influencing the internal life of the less developed countries, and so forth.

The question of cooperation of the developed countries with the less developed ones is particularly urgent in Africa and Asia, where economic weakness and underdevelopment not only retard the emancipation of the colonial countries and the attainment of their independence, but also hamstring, in one way or another, the independent development of those countries which have already formally acceded to independence, but whose political independence is often reduced to the lowest level by economic dependence. This is the actual substance of neo-colonialism, namely to retain its economic, and thereby also political positions, by maintaining a formally liberated country in a state of economic dependence on the metropolitan country. The same applies to the countries of Latin America; they are justly striving towards a more rapid economic development which they cannot easily achieve without appropriate international support and assistance.

The needs of underdeveloped regions are vast—and who is best in a position to give the necessary means to these regions? Naturally, the most developed countries, and primarily those which are spending, today, enormous resources on armaments. For these resources are not only being wasted for unproductive purposes, but are also the source of permanent tension and are causing mankind to live in fear of the possibility of an armed conflict. If only one-tenth of the resources that are being spent on armaments were invested into the development of less developed regions, this would meet the requirements of a very intensive development of those countries, whose peoples are suffering today great poverty and want. But this should be done without any political or similar conditions, because only in that case would cooperation be fully effective both in regard to the countries to be financed and in respect to the general improvement of the world situation. The overcoming of economic backwardness in Africa, Asia, and elsewhere would promote to the greatest extent the development of trade as well as general progress and prosperity in the world.

We are of the opinion that such cooperation can be insured in an appropriate manner and without discrimination through the United Nations. However, we feel that effective economic cooperation through bilateral channels should not be excluded. It goes without saying that concurrently with economic cooperation with underdeveloped countries, adequate technical cooperation in the form of the training of technical, scientific and other personnel should also be extended, so as to insure that economic resources are put to the best use. Although the technical assistance program of the United Nations has been increased to some extent, it is still far from satisfying actual needs. It is true that bilateral technical cooperation is being constantly increased. However, under the prevailing conditions of abnormal international relations, bilateral cooperation frequently embodies a considerable number of various negative elements, such as rivalry, interference in internal affairs, the imposing of political influence and the like. Therefore, sometimes this cooperation does more harm than good to the economically less developed countries. Nevertheless, without underestimating the importance of bilateral cooperation, I believe that scientific and technical assistance should be extended through the United Nations to a much greater extent than has been the case so far.

I expect that this conference will devote special attention to the question of economic cooperation among nonaligned countries. I am raising this question in view of the current international situation, which—owing to the division of the world into blocs—is increasingly obstructing economic cooperation and the closer linking up of the economies of various countries through the world market. The economy of each country, regardless of its social and economic system, feels the need of ever closer general economic cooperation. One of the greatest obstacles to closer economic relations and cooperation is the establishment of the Common Market in Western Europe and the recent setting up of the Organization for Economic Cooperation and Development (OECD), which is beginning to be referred to as the Atlantic Economic Community, then the establishment of the Council of Mutual Economic Assistance (SEV), the organization of East European countries, etc. For this reason, the countries outside these organizations, in the first place the nonaligned countries, find themselves subjected to discrimination. In the future, this situation could be even further aggravated, and could affect even more adversely the economic development of nonaligned as well as all other countries. For this reason, as well as many others, I feel that economic cooperation among the less developed countries should be established on the broadest possible basis and should include all the nonaligned countries as well as all the other less developed countries which are ready for such cooperation.

In my opinion such cooperation is necessary not with a view to establishing a new closed market, but precisely for the purpose of facilitating the elimination of obstacles and divisions in the world economy and helping all countries to participate in economic cooperation. This cooperation would not have a merely regional economic character, but also a broader, in a certain sense, universal one; at the same time, it would be, in addition to its economic importance, of a considerable general political significance.

I consider that the economic problems of the present-day world and, in the first place, the problems relating to cooperation with the less developed countries, deserve great attention on the part of the conference.

I have touched only upon some of the most important economic problems. However, the situation prevailing in world economic relations, and in the world market in particular, is extremely complex and constitutes one of the main causes of the many difficulties which are burdening international relations. The world market and economic relations in general are disrupted by the existence of various barriers and are replete with trends conducive to closed systems and exclusiveness. As a result of this, inter alia, there exists practically no universal economic organization in the present-day world. It would be of the greatest importance if not only the nonaligned countries, but all the forces in the world which are in favor of universal economic cooperation exerted greater efforts than heretofore for the establishment of universal economic organizations in the various sectors of economic activity, both within and outside the United Nations.

I feel that a world conference, at which all the most important economic questions would be considered, could facilitate a more effective approach to the solving of these problems.

Perhaps the most suitable place for the convening of such a meeting would be the United Nations.

I would like now to draw your attention to one more important question which is not only of interest to us but also to the whole world. Cooperation in the field of the use of atomic energy for peaceful purposes is becoming an important area of international cooperation. The strengthening of this cooperation, primarily with the less developed countries, would constitute, no doubt, a major contribution to international cooperation, not only from the economic, but also from every other point of view. In my opinion, the demand for a more equitable distribution and universal utilization of all scientific discoveries is fully justified, as they are actually the achievements of mankind as a whole.

V

Distinguished heads and representatives of states and governments, I believe that I can say without any exaggeration that the idea of constructive and peaceful co-existence among states with different internal social systems, as the only way to avoid the catastrophe of war, has gained broad support in the world. We could almost say that this idea has prevailed. Our country has gained, in this respect, a very positive experience in the course of a number of years, particularly in our relations with neighboring Greece and Italy, with whom we cooperate to our mutual satisfaction. It is sufficient to glance back and see what the relations between our countries were like ten years ago, in order to understand how useful and right were the broad-mindedness and good will with which both sides approached the problem of the consolidation of relations and establishment of constructive cooperation, regardless of differences in their social systems. From a source of possible conflicts, this area has been turned into an area of peace and peaceful cooperation. This applies also to our relations with many other countries, particularly with nonaligned countries. I know that all of you can quote similar examples and, therefore, I feel free to say that they fully confirm the value of the principles of peaceful and active co-existence among nations.

Active peaceful co-existence between various social systems is frequently interpreted in different ways. The practice and theory of co-existence seem different in different areas.

It is still widely believed that co-existence and cold war are part of a lasting state of international relations, particularly of the relations between blocs. Such views foreclose the prospect of a positive way out of the prevailing situation. Proceeding from such positions, certain circles in the world seem to believe that it is possible both to pursue a policy from a position of strength and to support co-existence. These are, however, two fundamentally different policies, which exclude one another. Further, the followers of such a policy consider that co-existence is only one of the bases for cooperation between states and peoples. We believe, however, that it is not one but the only basis under the present conditions, insuring positive cooperation and opening prospects for the gradual solution of burning contemporary problems.

Some consider co-existence to be merely a stratagem, which is quite suitable for some time as propaganda tactics, but that it is absurd to believe that the principle of co-existence could be adopted as something permanent in international relations in general, and between the Socialist and capitalist systems in particular. Some advocates of this view in the West are aware of the fact that should the principle of peaceful and active co-existence be adopted as a system in international relations, then—in a peaceful competition with the Socialist system— the capitalist system would not fare well. Therefore, they view co-existence with scepticism and claim that co-existence between Socialism and capitalism is not possible and that, sooner or later, an armed conflict and a final settling of accounts between them are inevitable, as the only way of preserving the capitalist system. Hence their insistence on force for the settlement of outstanding issues. Hence their uncompromising attitude towards progressive trends in the world, etc. These circles, even if they formally agree to talks on co-existence, wish to preserve the "status quo" in economic and social relations; they want to preserve the positions gained in the era of imperialism and colonialism. The assertion of the policy of co-existence does not mean that no further progressive processes and changes will take place in contemporary society, since co-existence is an integral part of these changes, which are historically ineluctable. Actually the policy of co-existence should insure that these changes be effected without war and that they be accompanied by a consolidation of democratic relations in the world and by a strengthening of the role of the broadest masses of people in the solving of economic and social problems.

On the other hand, there is also a theory that peaceful co-existence between blocs is possible. There is no doubt that even this, as a temporary solution in order to avoid a conflict, is better than war. But this is more like an armistice and we actually had such co-existence between the two world wars. It lasted in Europe for almost twenty years, until the Fascist powers succeeded in arming themselves to the teeth and in starting the Second World War, which caused enormous devastation and claimed millions of human lives.

There do not exist, however, only two blocs in the world. There is also a majority of countries not belonging to any bloc, which endorse peaceful and active co-existence as the only solution for avoiding the catastrophe of war. The question of peaceful co-existence should, therefore, be examined in a much broader framework, on a world scale. Peaceful co-existence should be implemented among states, and not only among states and peoples with different social systems but also among states and peoples with kindred systems. World peace is indivisible and, accordingly, wars are equally dangerous, no matter whether they break out between states with different internal systems or between states with identical or similar social systems. This was amply proved by the Second World War.

Wherein should lie the essence of peaceful and active co-existence? Armed conflict, as a means of settling accounts between states, is not the only concept which runs counter to peaceful co-existence; the "cold war," in all its variants, also makes constructive and peaceful cooperation impossible. Various forms of misinformation, mendacious and hostile propaganda in general, discrimination in relations among states, etc., are constantly poisoning the international atmosphere and creating a gulf between nations. There is no doubt that the arms race and the ever-present threat of a recourse to violent means, that is to say, to the force of arms for the settling of outstanding issues are the most important element of the cold war, but we must not overlook a practice that I have mentioned earlier in my speech, namely the various forms of psychological preparation based on the false, fabricated and offensive elements of cold war propaganda. All this is in flagrant contradiction with the essence of peaceful and active co-existence. The actual elimination of these negative cold war elements from international relations would create sound conditions for a broad and constructive cooperation among peoples, regardless of their internal social systems.

As regards internal social development in each individual country, it is a matter to be decided exclusively by the people concerned, depending on whether or not it wishes to maintain the capitalist social system or tends to build a Socialist system. Every people should be free to judge which system is more suitable for it. This has been proved quite clearly by present trends in Asian and African countries and by the tendency to advance towards Socialism gradually, in harmony with specific conditions and possibilities. The manner in which various peoples in capitalist countries will solve the question of their internal social system is entirely their own affair. The principle of peaceful and active co-existence has in fact become deeply rooted in actual practice. A clear proof of this is also provided by this historic gathering of the highest representatives of the peoples of nonaligned countries. The countries represented here have different internal social systems, but nevertheless they hold similar or identical views on the most important international problems of today. We hold also similar or identical views concerning the standards which should govern relations between states and peoples.

No one should foster the illusion that co-existence on an international scale can be attained by a mere declaration or resolution. It can be achieved only in practice, and its fundamental principles, fully elaborated, should be established by the United Nations, insofar as they are not yet incorporated in the Charter.

VI

What are our views on the United Nations and on the problem of its political strengthening and organizational consolidation?

Last year, a crisis arose in the United Nations in connection with events in the Congo. This crisis reached its climax at the Fifteenth Session of the General Assembly and has not yet been overcome as the question of the Congo still remains open. The situation prevailing today undoubtedly hampers the proper and effective functioning of the United Nations. Bearing in mind the extremely important role played by this international organization, particularly in the present difficult and abnormal situation, we cannot but be greatly concerned about its fate. Namely, if the present situation should continue, the consequences would be grave; it would not only reduce the

activities of the United Nations to a minimum of efficiency
but it could also endanger its very existence. I believe that the
solution of this crisis will also depend, to a great extent, on
the nonaligned countries, which had adopted a moderate and
constructive attitude at the Fifteenth Session of the General
Assembly already, and thus headed off a threat to the very existence of the United Nations. But that prevented the disaster
only temporarily and did not bring about a solution of the crisis.

I believe that we are, on the whole, in agreement that certain measures of reorganization should be undertaken in order
to enable the world organization to perform its functions more
successfully in the future and to eliminate the defects which
have appeared in the work of its organs, for example in the
case of the Congo. We must admit that, in spite of certain
weaknesses, the United Nations has played an important and
useful role by intervening in many disputes which constituted
a threat to peace, by preventing aggression, etc. Consequently,
we should make the greatest efforts to preserve this organization and enable it to carry out its responsible and difficult
functions in full.

I think that it is high time that the People's Republic of
China should take its seat in the United Nations, for it is
really absurd that a people of over six hundred million should
not have its representatives in that organization. It is just as
indispensable that other countries fulfilling the necessary requirements should also be admitted, so that the United Nations might really become a universal organization.

As far as the political strengthening of the United Nations
is concerned, it is, above all, essential to wage a resolute fight
against all tendencies to by-pass and weaken the organization
and to distort its role. It is necessary, at the same time, to influence, through and with the aid of the United Nations, the
course of international relations as effectively as possible in

the sense of peace and co-existence. This would not only mean, practically speaking, that the basic international issues should be settled in the United Nations, but also that they should be settled in such a way as to contribute both to the role and prestige of the organization itself and to the positive development of relations in the world. This should also mean that the resolutions of the United Nations should be implemented in a consistent manner and to the fullest extent. From the organizational point of view the structure of the United Nations should be adapted to the requirements of its activities under the present-day international conditions; it should be adapted to the changes which have taken place in international relations, along the further development of the fundamental principles of the Charter of the United Nations and the further strengthening and democratization of the organization.

One of the most urgent tasks is the extension of the membership of some of the principal organs of the United Nations, namely of the Security Council and the Economic and Social Council, so as to bring the structure of the membership of these more restricted bodies into harmony with the considerably increased membership of the United Nations and to enable all the new members—and this means primarily the regions of the world in Asia and Africa which have been neglected so far—to assert themselves fully and to exercise in these organs the influence to which they are entitled.

We should also endeavor to further strengthen the role of the General Assembly as a broad democratic and, in the full sense of the word, representative organ of the United Nations.

As regards the question of the Secretary-General and of the Secretariat of the United Nations, which has recently acquired particular urgency, a certain revision and adaptation should also be carried out in this field but, in our opinion, not in a way which would amount to a freezing of present divisions in the world. I think, first of all, that the role of the Secretary-

General should be brought back within the framework provided for under the Charter, according to which he is only an administrative officer of the United Nations and has no independent political powers. In actual practice, for various reasons, this has all too often not been the case.

Concurrently with this, it is necessary to take concrete measures for the purpose of reorganizing the machinery of the Secretariat of the United Nations in such a manner as to provide a safeguard that the Secretary-General will act within the limits of his responsibilities. At the same time, the structure of the Secretariat should be brought into harmony with the changed, that is to say, with the new relationships in the United Nations and in the world. Perhaps this could be achieved, through the establishment, alongside the Secretary-General, of a consultative body consisting of, say, five or more members, which would, in assisting the Secretary-General, insure a proper interpretation of the recommendations and decisions of the appropriate organs of the United Nations.

While speaking of this, we constantly bear in mind the fact that the weakening of the United Nations would have an extremely negative effect upon the general development of international relations. It would deal a harsh blow upon these relations taken as a whole and particularly to the interests of small and newly-liberated countries, for whom the United Nations is becoming to an increasing extent a supreme form of the international community and guarantor of the equal rights of all peoples and countries, large and small. Furthermore, we should bear in mind that the major international problems of the present-day world, which are increasing the dangers inherent in the world situation, cannot be solved without the United Nations.

VII

Mr. Chairman, If we proceed from the standpoint of outstanding problems on which the nonaligned countries lay emphasis in the interest of peace, constructive cooperation and the future of mankind, we observe that this conference is the direct result of many experiences and lessons learned by all of us. At the same time, it provides a proof of our determination to shoulder that part of the responsibility for peace and for the fate of the world that we have to bear under the present circumstances.

The negative development of international relations and a tendency towards further tension and crises at the most sensitive points make it impossible to undertake, in a serious manner, the solution of outstanding and acute problems in those areas of the world where many peoples still suffer under the yoke of colonialism, under the burden of want, backwardness and various forms of discrimination as well as new forms of interference and domination from outside. The maintenance and aggravation of the cold war and recurring crises inevitably divert the attention of the world from the urgent problems of dependent and less developed regions and countries. The efforts aimed at a timely solution of these problems are thereby obstructed and paralyzed, which cannot but prolong the state of uncertainty and instability of peace in these regions as well.

We have assembled here at a difficult time, at a fateful moment for the future of world peace.

Our material resources are modest and our possibilities are far from being limitless, but our moral power is immense, and this is of paramount importance today. Not only the peoples of our countries, but also public opinion throughout the world expect much of us. Their eyes are turned in our direction with expectation and trust. Furthermore, our good will and determination to place all our resources and abilities in the service of a better future for our countries and for the world in which we live know no boundaries and can surmount all obstacles.

When we have embarked upon an independent role, not aligning ourselves with the groupings of countries in the two opposing camps, and when we resisted the policy of the division of the world and rejected all that it entails—we have chosen an arduous road. Nevertheless, we had the strength to embark upon and to persevere along the road, propagating and implementing a program of peace and co-existence which is today widely known and recognized in the world. Thanks to this road we have been able to make and we are still increasing our contribution to the common cause. It is in the name of this program and of our firm resolution to increase our contribution still further that we have assembled here today in order to coordinate our forces, to unite our efforts and to help the world—which is constantly being pushed to the brink of disaster—to become conscious, even at this late hour, of all the dangers that threaten it, to mobilize its vast moral forces and energy towards the consolidation of world peace and the extension of general international cooperation on an equal footing.

IX

Address on Current International and Domestic Issues

Leskovac, Yugoslavia
October 20, 1968

Following herewith is the complete text of President Tito's address in which he analyzes the domestic and foreign issues facing Yugoslavia in 1968, and strongly rebukes the Soviet Union and the other Warsaw Pact nations for their invasion and occupation of the Czechoslovak Socialist Republic.

IX

International and Domestic Issues

Comrades: May I first extend to you the warmest greetings of all of us who have come to this magnificent gathering, and our thanks for the cordial reception and welcome you have prepared for us. I am happy to have the opportunity to be among you again, although only after fifteen years. I say this with some self-criticism, but my job is such that I cannot always go where and when I wish.

I especially want to greet the surviving fighters of the majestic struggle that our people waged against every invader, and to express to them once more our thanks for the fact that today, again, when our country is in the full swing of constructing a Socialist society, they are so active.

We can today say that, despite all the obstacles and difficulties that have confronted us during the past more than twenty

years, our Yugoslavia has been transformed. It is no longer
what it was. It is today an advanced, industrially developed
country with many new buildings, schools, hospitals, and
other projects. This is a country where the people view the
past with pride and look with faith to the future in creating
everything that our people has always desired.

Let me turn now to this year, which has had some stormy
days. First of all, we have drawn up a balance from the past
two or three years of economic and social reform. And we
have had good results. I can say that, in spite of all the difficulties we have encountered during these three years since we
started the economic reform, we have also had very good successes. This year has especially shown very vital activity in all
fields of our internal life. This year, too, our youth has raised
a powerful voice in a desire to join with all who are building
Socialism, with the same rights and the same duties. We have
accepted all the justified criticism which has come from the
young people and from the working class.

I must say that never in the past more than twenty years
has Yugoslavia demonstrated such unity as has been the case
this year. The unity of our peoples and our youth, the unity of
our wish to preserve our unhindered development, our Socialist construction, to defend our independence from any attempt
to interfere in our internal affairs, has been powerfully dis-
played.

This year, as you know, there have been grave excesses on
the international scene. I did not mean to speak about Czechoslovakia, because enough has been said on that subject. I
would only like to say that, as in 1948 when we were directly
touched, we have now again said a decisive "No!" Our position, our views on the Czechoslovak case have been made
clear to the whole world, and we stand by them forever. I believe that the principles of noninterference, independence, integrity, and sovereignty must be valid for all countries of the
world, whether they be members of a bloc or not.

This policy of ours provoked a revolt among some of our friends and neighbors in the Eastern countries—Poland, the Soviet Union, Hungary, the Democratic Republic of Germany, and especially Bulgaria. And, of course, they again began, as they had in 1948, to attack our country in the press and in speeches. We, naturally, must reply when principles are involved. I believe—and I must emphasize this today—that our press should not answer them with the same language. It should reply only on matters of principle, and treat them as laid down in the Program of the League of Communists, and generally in accordance with the views of our peoples. Picking on trifles can only damage us, but reply we must.

Let us take, for example, the way the situation in Yugoslavia is depicted in some Eastern countries. We are amazed that the leaders—I do not mean the people—of these countries can so falsely present conditions in our country, saying we have failed with self-management, that our internal system is no good, that our people beg in the streets, that our children are naked, etc. These are crass lies which our people must really indignantly refute. It is said, further, that we are in debt, that we have, so to speak, sold out to the West, that this is no longer even Socialism, that we are moving toward capitalism. You know these attacks very well.

In our dialogue with them, I have told them: Twenty million tourists from all over the world have traveled throughout Yugoslavia this year. Twenty million tourists have best seen what our people are like, how they live, what we have accomplished. Especially those who had previously been in our country have been able to see the enormous changes here. Those who have visited Yugoslavia have denied all the slanders that have been cast at our country.

Comrades, this is not a matter of an incidental, insignificant dispute between us and them. This is simply the fact that they do not like our social system, our self-governing Socialist system, our path of Socialism and Communism. They do not like our Socialist democracy. They are particularly disturbed by our self-management, and therefore they have now attacked our internal system. But this will not upset us much. We shall show them the facts of our achievements.

They attack our reform even though they themselves seek ways toward some kind of reform.

These then, are some of the basic elements which now stand between them and us. And in the case of Czechoslovakia, the main point, in my opinion, was precisely the fact that the social development of that country had taken a democratic path toward changes which would have made it easier for the people to create a better life.

I would now like to return to what we have so far achieved in the economic reform. First, with many difficulties we have still done an enormous amount. You can see for yourselves that we have stabilized our dinar. The dinar today is of value in the world. Wherever you go today you can use the dinar.

We have also stabilized prices. True, prices here and there have risen, but in the main it can be said that prices have stabilized, and this despite the serious efforts we must invest in implementing the economic reform.

We have already modernized about 55 per cent of our industry, and we have done much toward introducing automation. This is a great advance.

We have almost settled our balance of payments. Only a small difference remains, while up to three years ago we had a deficit of 250 million dollars. We have increased our exports by 50 per cent. This, of course, is still not enough. We must do still more to increase exports because our industry today is not working at full capacity. In this area there are still great and unused possibilities.

We have made great progress in agricultural production. You can feel that yourselves. And what does this mean? We can today satisfy all our food needs from our own agriculture.

It is no longer necessary for us to import wheat. We are now producing sufficient wheat, corn, and other agricultural products. There are, however, difficulties in the sense that the agricultural products we have for export meet very serious competition obstacles on foreign markets. This is particularly true of exports of corn, livestock, meat, etc. We are now endeavoring to arrive at an arrangement with Western markets, that is, with the European Common Market, which would enable us to sell our agricultural products on those markets, without the so-called *prélèvement* and other restrictions.

Our industry is largely modernized. It has already adapted itself to new market conditions. The best evidence of this is that our industry has ceased producing around 10,000 various articles which were out of date, and turned to the production of about 15,000 new items that are of interest both to foreign markets and at home. This required great efforts. We had to tighten our belts to a considerable extent. When we talk about our progress we must not, of course, lose sight of our weaknesses. In so far as the further modernization of our industry is concerned, we must still do a great deal and at a still faster pace.

Our productivity is increasing by about 6 per cent per year. That is good, but we must increase it still further. We have gone from a forty-eight-hour to a forty-two-hour working week, while at the same time we have raised productivity, primarily by orientation toward modernization and more intensive work. The question now arises, where will the workers go who have had to leave the factories because modernization has taken away their jobs. Our government, and all of us in leading positions, are making great efforts to solve the problem of unemployment in a way that will gradually and persistently open up new jobs, organize new projects, improve our infrastructure, which we have already planned for this year. It will be possible to employ tens of thousands of workers. There are also other matters to be settled, such as, for example, the additional part-time jobs.

Regardless of what some people abroad say about us, the facts show that our standard of living is rising annually by 10 per cent. We still, of course, have many things to correct, and we must advance more quickly, because, there is still much to do to attain the goals we have set ourselves in the economic reform.

Some in the East criticize our system and conditions in our country. But let us look at the phases through which we have passed in the last twenty years. In 1948, the Soviet Union and other East European countries simply cancelled unilaterally all agreements with Yugoslavia. We found ourselves, so to speak, naked on the road. Our country had been destroyed. We had enormous casualties during the war and suffered from terrible consequences of the war destruction. We had no friends in the West at that time. What remained to us then? To sell ourselves or to find a better way? First, we called upon our people to tighten their belts, to apply themselves more energetically to their work with the same unity and persistence they had shown in the National Liberation War. Then we inquired in the West whether someone would grant us credit. In the West they said: All right, we will give you credit but on very difficult terms. They asked for interest of even up to 10 per cent. They also required us first to pay off the debts of old Yugoslavia. They told us: Pay for those tiny factories that we built in Yugoslavia. The mines and factories had been in the hands of foreign capitalists. What could we do then? We told them: All right, we accept, we will pay the debts of old Yugoslavia; we will pay you compensation for the nationalized factories and mines and we will take the credit on the terms you dictate.

For many years our country remained in isolation by the East European countries. We proceeded step by step in taking credit from the West. And by 1960 we had paid off all the pre-war debts which we acknowledged as our obligation to foreign countries. This, of course, meant tremendous efforts for our people. It demanded austerity, and often the denial of the most elementary everyday needs. But we overcame all the difficulties. At that time our stores had no, or practically no, goods, and what they did have was not of the best quality. But look at our country today. Those same people who criticize us and say we have nothing, come here to buy goods. Yes, that is lying propaganda which will not harm us. In fact it will do more damage to them.

The question now arises, how shall we react to these not exactly friendly, in fact slanderous, attitudes toward our country. I believe that these false presentations of the situation in our country can damage only them and not us. For thousands and thousands of people from these countries have already been in Yugoslavia and have marveled at the way we have been able, so quickly, to pull ourselves out of the ruins and achieve such results. In fact, this has been admired by the entire world. I do not say that everything in our country is all it should be. We still have people who live badly, who are poorly paid. But we shall eliminate that, too. You can be sure that we shall overcome all difficulties if we work with such persistence and unity.

Consequently, comrades, when we ask what should be our attitude toward all these attacks, I think it must be such that no stain falls upon us of provoking anybody or of wishing to impair relations. On the contrary, we constantly insist: Let us cooperate at least where it is possible, in economic and other similar fields.

In so far as we are concerned, we desire good relations. But, as you know, good relations do not depend on only one side, they always depend on both sides.

I have mentioned several countries which do not take a particularly friendly attitude toward us. Now I would like to

say something about our nearest neighbor, Bulgaria. You
know that, three years ago, I visited Bulgaria. Also, the President of the Bulgarian Government, Todor Zivkov, visited Yugoslavia. At that time we discussed the need to eliminate elements that could disturb our friendly relations. We agreed not
to attack one another. We agreed that anything concerning Macedonia was a matter for the Macedonian people and nobody
else.

However, even after that agreement the Bulgarian press, as
it had done previously, continued to say that the Bulgarian
Army took part in the liberation of Yugoslavia, that the Yugoslav National Liberation Army had not been able to do anything very much. Thus, they belittle the struggle of our peoples. I therefore want to say here what I think of this.

In 1944, toward the end of the war, when I went from Vis
to Craiova, Rumania, from where I later left for Belgrade, I
received a Bulgarian delegation which included Comrades
Terpesev and Todorov. They asked me, as Commander-in-Chief and President of the National Committee—the government at that time—to make it possible for the Bulgarian
Army, which had previously been under Fascist command, to
participate with us in the liberation of the remaining part of
our territory. They said they were ashamed, that their people
had been misled, and that the participation of their army in
such an operation would be very beneficial to them. I agreed,
and Bulgarian units took part in those battles alongside our
units. Here is what the Central Committee of the Bulgarian
Communist Party wrote at that time. Their letter of November 2, 1944, says:

> The Yugoslav National Liberation Army which you organized
> and which you lead has done an enormous service both in the
> liberation of our dismembered fatherland and in dealing a serious
> blow to Hitler's bands in the Balkans and driving them out. The
> Yugoslav peoples, and in the first place the brave neighboring
> Serbian people, were the first to raise the flag in a decisive Na-

tional Liberation struggle against Hitler's Germany and to show to all the enslaved and subject peoples the road to freedom. Your shining example also inspired and taught our deceived and plundered people to wage an armed Partisan struggle against the Hitlerite and Bulgarian agents. . . .

Our people have a feeling of guilt toward the Yugoslav peoples, especially toward the Serbs and Macedonians, for having permitted our Fascist rulers to make Bulgaria a military base for German invaders, to make the Bulgarian Army Hitler's gendarmes in the Balkans, and to carry out acts of armed force and treason against peoples fighting for their freedom.

Our people, who themselves have felt the horror of violence and treason perpetrated by Bulgarian leaders who sold out to Hitler, against fighters for freedom, are ready to do all they can to erase, as much and as soon as possible, the memory of what has just passed, and to clear the way to a lasting, unbreakable partnership, a close fraternal alliance with all the Yugoslav peoples. . . . We owe you our eternal gratitude for your support and brotherly assistance in enabling us to form our first Partisan units in your country.

There you are. That is what the Central Committee of the Bulgarian Communist Party wrote when Comrade Dimitrov was at its head. On the basis of this, representatives of the National Committee of the National Liberation of Yugoslavia, in cordial and friendly talks with Dobre Terpesev and Petar Todorov, reached an agreement, on October 5, 1944, the text of which included the following:

Agreement has been reached:
1) On military cooperation in the struggle against the common enemy, the German conqueror;
2) That all questions arising from the allied relationship and the friendly cooperation of Bulgaria and Yugoslavia will be settled in the spirit of brotherhood and the common interests of the peoples of Yugoslavia and Bulgaria.

Delegates of the Bulgarian National Front have expressed their readiness to do everything to correct the wrongs done to the peoples of Yugoslavia by the reactionary Fascist elements in the Bulgarian Government, and to exert every effort toward the normalization of relations between the Bulgarian and Yugoslav peoples in the spirit of full and brotherly solidarity.

There is more of this, but I shall not read any more; it is not necessary. But, comrades, the blood was so fresh then, it was, so to speak, still steaming, and nobody could dispute the tremendous casualties we had suffered in the war. But today, you see, these casualties are being disputed. At that time foundations of friendship and brotherly relations between Yugoslavia and Bulgaria were laid. Today these foundations are again being destroyed by various historical distortions, nonrecognition of Macedonian nationality, etc. What are you Marxist Bulgarian leaders thinking of? It is emphasized in Marxist-Leninist science that every nation has the right to self-determination, to secession.

Today, however, they deny even the nationality of the Macedonian people, not to mention their right to self-determination in accordance with their own internal development and life.

As you see, these are the elements that now burden our relations with Bulgaria. Let them return to the situation as it was at the beginning of 1944, when we fought side by side. We extended our hand to them then, and never for one moment have we withdrawn it. We do not withdraw it today either. We desire good relations with the Bulgarian people, but we also want them to respect the historic events, to respect the victims of that common fight in 1944, toward the end of the war against the Fascist invaders.

From this spot—and I am sure you will approve—despite all that has happened between us in recent times, I emphàsize: Let us go forward together. Let us offer a hand, one to the other, because we have many possibilities of cooperation. Can there be stability in the Balkans if there is not friendship and good relations between Yugoslavia and Bulgaria? Clearly there cannot. Cooperation between Yugoslavia and Bulgaria should be the foundation stone of stability in the Balkans. That is what we desire, because we would like to build a better life in peace. I think the Bulgarian people, too, desire it. I must say, however, that the recent statement by one of the top leaders of Bulgaria asserting that all Socialist countries have an obligation to help when Socialism is in danger in a certain country, is unacceptable and contrary to the principle of a country's sovereignty. It emerges from this statement that they would even come to Yugoslavia to "help," and without our invitation. If they did they would get a very rough welcome! If you are not invited it means that you are not needed. In so far as we are concerned, we settle our own internal affairs ourselves. Socialism in our country is in no danger whatsoever. All our people live in the spirit of Socialist construction. Socialism has deep roots in Yugoslavia which nobody can uproot. Nobody need have any fear that someone from the West could encroach upon our independence. We are sufficiently free to defend our country from anyone who attempts anything against us.

Comrades, when I speak like this it may look as though I am dramatizing the matter. Not in the least! There is no dramatization whatever in this. I only wanted to say openly what we think, to remind them to look back to what has been, because, it seems, they have forgotten everything. It is good for them to be reminded a little. For we no longer hear them mention today all that the Bulgarian Fascists did, especially in this area. And they even went further than this—all the way to Zlatibor. Their guns fired on us during our withdrawal in the fifth offensive when we were in a most difficult situation. This, it appears, they have forgotten, but they should not forget. Because we cannot forget our casualties. And those who were our opponents then, ought to keep this in mind for the future as well.

Comrades, in an attempt to justify somehow the Czechoslovak case—that is the invasion by troops of the five Socialist countries—a certain theory has been expressed that sovereignty is not essential for small nations. Small nations were not precisely mentioned, but this is what it means. In this way they, in fact, try to legalize something which is completely untenable, which does not exist even in the Atlantic Charter or anywhere else.

We do not hear this even from the capitalist countries which, in view of their concepts, would not be so surprising. But we do hear it, unfortunately, from some leaders of Socialist countries, and that is a very difficult and serious matter. The principles of sovereignty and integrity have existed for centuries. We must therefore sharply refute such theories. In the dialogues we have with the leading comrades of the Socialist countries on these questions, we shall dispute them, and our press should write about this. But they should not insist on trifles which can only make our position in such discussions more difficult.

The situation in the world at present is very unclear. And I believe that the recent events in Czechoslovakia have contributed much to making the situation worse than it was.

What should we in Yugoslavia do? What is our task? Our duty, in the first place, is to pay the maximum attention to our internal development so that we can best solve any problems that confront us. But, at the same time, we must with the same alertness follow what happens outside our country. Yugoslavia enjoys great prestige in the world. There are few countries today that do not know of the struggle of the Yugoslav people, or what Yugoslavia has contributed to peace and progress, there are few countries that are not acquainted with the principles of Yugoslav foreign policy and her views on relations among nations.

We have again taken the initiative for convening a summit meeting of the nonaligned countries with a wish to make it more extensive than the ones held in Belgrade and Cairo. This initiative, which is not ours alone, has met with a very poor reception among the leaders of some Socialist countries. Previously the Western capitalists were against it. The Western imperialist states did not like the idea and now it is the others who do not like it. Meanwhile, everywhere, particularly in Africa and Asia, invented stories are being circulated that this is a lost cause, that Yugoslavia has failed with this idea, that it has damaged Yugoslavia itself, that there is no longer any sense in proposing a meeting. This means an attempt to persuade statesmen and responsible people not to attend such a meeting because in international relations negative elements are piling up and the world is increasingly burdened with very acute problems which could again lead to a world catastrophe.

On two occasions in recent years, I have visited several countries in Asia and Africa. With the exception of Japan which is, of course, a highly developed country, I visited mainly the developing countries. Wherever I went the leaders and responsible people accepted with both hands the idea of the need for such a meeting. What shall we discuss at that meeting?

The world, as I say, is faced with a difficult dilemma, with grave conflicts. It is difficult to solve international problems in the UN. Almost no acute international question has been settled. The crisis in the Middle East caused by Israel's attack on the UAR and other Arab countries has not been solved. The aggressive war in Vietnam has not been ended, although in recent days there has been talk that the negotiations have taken a somewhat better turn. There have been rumors for years of various settlements, but the problems are still not solved, and there are more and more hotbeds which could provoke very serious conflicts.

I am unable to say that in the Middle East—which touches Europe, and particularly us here in the Mediterranean—that there will not be another grave armed conflict which would not be confined merely to the directly concerned countries, but could also spread to European countries. That is why we are very worried, and why I think it necessary to have a meeting of the developing countries and countries threatened by the big powers. This situation will certainly also be reflected now in other Western countries. They can say: If they (the Socialist countries) do not respect sovereignty, why should we respect it? Small countries, consequently, are in danger. For this reason small countries should act in unity. Their representatives at such a meeting should clearly and decisively say that no one has the right to interfere in their internal affairs. Small countries have the right to defend their sovereignty with determination. They have the right to seek help in their development, because various colonial powers have plundered their countries for, not decades, but centuries. They have the right to seek the preservation of world peace, the liquidation of atomic and other armaments, and the abolition of force as a means of solving international problems.

These, comrades, are serious matters that directly affect not only us but many countries of the world. We shall, therefore, stubbornly fight for the convening of such a meeting.

What, now, are our prospects? As for the economic reform, I believe that we have mastered the most difficult part. Our affairs are now progressing better and better. The prospects, as we see them, are not bad. We have increasingly broad possibilities for a still more rapid economic and social development. We are now proceeding at an accelerated tempo toward the further modernization of our industry, the construction of new transport communications, the development of our infrastructure, etc. We are endeavoring to expand our foreign trade. Our people who go abroad must be more skillful in studying the markets so that they may know how to do business to the advantage of our country and to the advantage of those to whom we sell our goods and services.

We are engaged in considerable business in many countries of Africa and Asia. Yugoslavia, as you know, has so far given about 650 million dollars in credit, some of which has already been repaid to us. We are building factories, ports, delivering ships, carrying out drilling operations, finding water in the desert, and so on. In other words, our experts have achieved renown in whatever country they have worked. Wherever I have been I have heard words of praise for our experts and our workers. Everyone emphasizes that they are capable and good people. Many of our doctors are working abroad. We have today so many skilled people that we are in a position to aid countries with insufficient qualified personnel. And that is not all. Our workers and experts are working in the highly developed countries also. We are, for example, engaged in construction works in Germany, Czechoslovakia and other countries of Europe. Comrades in Czechoslovakia spoke most favorably of our experts. It appears likely that we shall be engaged in new extensive construction work in Czechoslovakia. Our comrades there want us to build 10,000 apartments. We can accept this work because we have sufficient qualified people to do it. The contract has not yet been signed.

Because of our reputation, our experts and workers have no difficulty breaking through in the world. They are well received everywhere, especially in the developing countries such as those of Africa and Asia. In this, therefore, our prospects are very good.

Many of our people have gone to work in West Germany, France, Switzerland, Sweden, etc. You must not think, however, that all these people were unemployed. A number of qualified people from our factories, where they were needed, also went abroad. But they went abroad to earn more money so that they could more easily buy an automobile, and so on. How they lived there, however, is another question.

Diplomatic relations between our country and the Federal

Republic of Germany had been broken off. On their initiative, these relations have been re-established without the imposition of any conditions whatsoever. They broke off relations but they gave the initiative for the restoration of these relations. And now, when we again have diplomatic relations, we are proceeding to settle the problems that exist between us. Yugoslav workers in Germany had none of the rights accorded to workers from other countries, such as Turkey, Italy, etc., not to mention the rights enjoyed by German workers. We have now succeeded in obtaining a favorable settlement for these people including the question of pensions and insurance. Yugoslav workers have obtained the same status as German workers. This was a major problem for us.

It would, of course, be better if we were able to employ all our people at home. But, that possibility does not exist yet. We shall, however, create the possibility. The question of unemployment is not easy, it must be solved gradually. I have already said that modernization makes possible an accelerated accumulation, with many fewer workers. Now it is necessary to find new jobs for this labor surplus which is leaving the factories because of modernization and automation. This needs careful study and a fundamental approach. We are firmly determined to solve this problem, too.

In conclusion, I thank you once more for your patience in listening to me. I wish you much success in your further creative efforts.

X

Address to the Jubilee Session of the Anti-Fascist Council of the National Liberation of Yugoslavia— the Twenty-Fifth Anniversary of The New Yugoslavia

Jajce, Yugoslavia
November 30, 1968

Following herewith is the complete text of President Tito's historic address commemorating the first quarter-century of New Yugoslavia.

X

Twenty-Fifth Anniversary Address

Comrades, dear guests: A quarter of a century ago, in the heart of enslaved Europe, while all the Allies were fighting major battles against the Hitlerite coalition and our National Liberation Army was locked in combat with the forces of occupation and domestic traitors, true representatives of the people of all parts of Yugoslavia met here to give legal form to their attainments—cemented by the blood of the best sons and daughters of our peoples—in both the military and political spheres, which had found expression a year earlier as well, at the First Session of the Anti-Fascist Council of the National Liberation of Yugoslavia (AFCNLY) in Bihać. The Second Session of the AFCNLY was of historic significance for the destiny of our peoples. It reflected the revolutionary aspiration of all of them for the establishment of a new state, a free and democratic community of equal peoples and nationalities of Yugoslavia. The decisions which then constituted the AFCNLY as the supreme legislative and representative body were far-reaching in their significance, as they formed the basis of the sovereignty and statehood of the new Yugoslavia. Also of major importance was the decision to form the National Committee as the executive organ, that is, as the government of the new Yugoslavia.

The desire of our peoples to live in a community based on equality, which came to the fore so powerfully during the National Liberation War, goes far back into the past. It had long been the wish of the most progressive men and women of all our peoples, and particularly of those who had fought for decades against the domination of Austro-Hungary.

The events of fifty years ago were in no case the result of any kind of illusion or fiction about the ethnical relationship between the South Slav peoples. They had deep roots both in that ethnical relationship, and in the natural processes which had brought the South Slav peoples closer together and provided links between them; these peoples had, owing to their geographic and economic position, and their relatively small numbers, found themselves in a special position, common to all of them, in relation to the world centers of political, economic and military power.

Unfortunately, however, the state created by the unification following the First World War, after the collapse of the former Austro-Hungarian Monarchy, brought disillusionment to our peoples in terms of their real aspirations. The former Yugoslavia was not the kind of state wanted and imagined by the most honest patriots and fighters for unification, or by the masses of the people, when Yugoslavia was being created. The imperialists and domestic capitalists made of it the kind of state they needed. The popular name for it was the "Versailles Yugoslavia," for it was at Versailles that its size and form had been tailored. It was the result of an assault by the reactionary bourgeoisie of Yugoslavia against the working masses who had been caught up in a wave of revolution. The working masses also fought against national intolerance and against Greater-Serbian bourgeois hegemony; they fought for their fundamental economic, social and national rights. The Croatian and Slovenian bourgeoisies, frightened by the revolutionary mood of the broad masses of the people who sincerely desired unity—a mood which had spread as an echo of the October Revolution—were quick to find a common language with the Greater-Serbian bourgeoisie, and that language meant exploitation and deprivation for the working people of Yugoslavia; it meant that the best sons of the people were thrown into prison; it meant the outlawing of the Communist Party, and so on.

A community was thus set up in a manner and on foundations and principles that the people had neither expected nor desired. Not much time had to pass for it to become clear that the age-old progressive desire for unification had been completely betrayed. It was soon obvious that this was a construction in which anti-people's regimes played traitor to the genuine interests of the people and in which the social exploitation of the working people by the young and insatiable bourgeoisie was worse than it had ever been before. At the same time, the new state, under the hegemony of the Greater-Serbian bourgeoisie, supported all along by one clique or another of the Croatian and Slovenian bourgeoisies had built up a centralistic and unitaristic system; it was, from the very first day of its existence, a country of national oppression.

Pregnant with numerous antagonisms from the very beginning, rent asunder by the incitement of national hatred, by brutal exploitation and the corruption that burgeoned at the top, pre-war Yugoslavia quickly fell prey to foreign capitalist monopolies. National betrayal by the bourgeoisie and the top ruling circles generally, before the war and during the first days of the Fascist onslaught against this country, was the logical conclusion of the traitorous role the Yugoslav bourgeoisie and the ruling cliques had played during the entire existence of the former Yugoslavia, selling out the interests of our peoples to the foreign imperialists.

This conclusion and betrayal were, however, simultaneously one of the factors figuring most significantly in the political isolation of the bourgeoisie from the great majority of the masses. Under those conditions, it was inevitable that the National Liberation War, participated in by the broad masses of peasants, headed by the working class and led by the Communist Party, would end not only in the liberation of the country from the occupation forces but also in the loss of power by the treacherous bourgeoisie and the destruction of its anti-people's regime, headed by the king.

The Communist Party of Yugoslavia, which had, long before the occupation, pointed out that the danger of Fascism was growing which had carried out comprehensive preparations for defending the country, was in a position to lead the people into an armed uprising against the foreign Fascist occupiers. It succeeded in doing so as the National Liberation movement had from its very inception fought under the slogan both of national liberation, brotherhood and unity, and the creation of a genuinely democratic order in the new Yugoslavia under which the will of the broad masses would truly find expression. The people joined the struggle *en masse* because they did not want to see a reversion to the old order, because they had finally become convinced of the betrayal of the ruling bourgeoisie, because they wished to rid the country of all occupiers as soon as possible, because they wanted to prevent mutual extermination and because the Communist Party of Yugoslavia had from the very beginning opened up vistas of the establishment of a new community of equal peoples in which they would be the masters of their fate. The party succeeded because it had, from the very first day of the insurrection, considered one of the most important and fateful questions to be the task of forging brotherhood and unity among the peoples of Yugoslavia, as well as unity among the masses of each individual people and nationality. The National Liberation struggle brought with it freedom, brotherhood and equality for all the peoples and nationalities of Yugoslavia, and that is truly one of the greatest achievements of our revolution.

Consequently, the basic feature of our people's revolution is that it was from its very inception invested with the character of a liberation war against the occupiers and at the same time of a struggle for new social relationships, for the proper solution of the national question, for a more just social system.

The people's uprising spread quickly throughout all parts of Yugoslavia. Whenever we lost one area, we liberated another, thereby insuring the influx of new fighting men and the strengthening of the people's army. Thus, the enemy, no matter what superiority in numbers he enjoyed, was never able to cover the entire territory of our country, to weaken the striking power of the people's struggle and revolution. Conditions were thereby created, and this had been demonstrated as necessary, for the formation of larger military units. In the autumn of 1943, we had 300,000 fighting men in the brigades and divisions and in the many Partisan detachments. Irrespective of our army's numerical strength, however, we kept on engaging the far more powerful enemy. The best testimony to this is the fact that we kept roughly forty-five divisions of occupation forces pinned down in our country during the entire war. This simultaneously attests the great contribution made by the struggle of our peoples to the cause of the Allies and all democratic, freedom-loving and anti-imperialist forces.

Parallel with the development of the National Liberation

struggle and the National Liberation movement, as early as 1941, as a form of revolutionary alliance of the working peoples, the People's Liberation committees began emerging from that movement both in liberated and unliberated areas, as the first embryos of the revolutionary people's power. Even then, under the most difficult imaginable wartime conditions, many forms of direct democracy found expression in the functioning of these committees, from elections and the right of recall, to broad participation by the citizens in the making and implementation of decisions. Through such democratic-revolutionary practice, the committees were quick to assert themselves as genuine organs of people's power, as a reflection of direct people's sovereignty.

It was this essentially that predetermined the entire course of our revolution as Socialist, while its intermeshing with National Liberation and revolutionary-democratic elements gave it the specific political forms through which it manifested itself.

I do not think it necessary, this time, to describe the entire course of our revolution and to enumerate all of its elements. But even the foregoing suffices to show that our revolution was authentic, that it had an all-people's and a genuinely democratic character. It reflected the interests of each one of our peoples and of all of them together. The revolution in Yugoslavia was no copy of outside models and schemas. It had a broad base in the masses of the people, above all in the young people, in the mass organization of the National Liberation Front the ideological and political nucleus of which was provided by the working class, with the Communist Party playing the undisputed and generally recognized leading role. From the very beginning, our revolution took as its point of departure the principle that the free will of each people and each nationality would have to come fully to expression.

It was therefore not by accident that, even before the constituting of the AFCNLY as the supreme legislative body, national political bodies had been established, that is, the councils of National Liberation, for the areas of the present republics and provinces, which also exercised the prerogatives of government organs. This means that the foundations of a federal system, of an equal community of peoples, associated on a voluntary basis, had been laid even then.

The decisions passed by the Second Session of the AFCNLY actually came as the result of decisions taken by the representative bodies of the various peoples of Yugoslavia, prior to the session in Jajce.

The legal foundations of the federal state community, and thereby also the basis for its sovereignty and integrity, were laid at the Second Session of the AFCNLY.

The Declaration of the Second Session confirmed the Leninist principle of the right of peoples to self-determination, including the right to secession. The decisions of that session stressed that no one other than the peoples of Yugoslavia could make decisions about the internal system of the country, by which the AFCNLY demonstrated its determined opposition to any and all forms of foreign intervention and interference in the country's internal affairs. This determination was also reflected in the demand that the Allies respect the freely expressed will of the peoples of Yugoslavia and stop supporting the government-in-exile.

At this historic gathering, the principle was proclaimed of the continuity of the Yugoslav state in the international community, which the peoples of Yugoslavia had confirmed in practice in the common struggle for liberation. This common struggle reflected the determination of all the peoples of Yugoslavia to remain firmly united, on a basis of equality, in the defense of their integrity; to refuse to recognize that anyone had the right to dismember Yugoslavia. The AFCNLY also confirmed the decisions of the Slovenian National Liberation

Committee and of the AFCNL of Croatia regarding the desire of the people in the area of the Slovenian coast, Istria, Rijeka, Zadar and the islands to join their mother country, manifested through mass participation by the people of these regions in the National Liberation struggle.

The new Yugoslavia, which emerged from the flames of the Liberation War, started out on the difficult and complicated road of struggle for international affirmation and recognition. An important relevant document was the note sent by the executive committee of the AFCNLY and the Supreme HQ, even before the Jajce session, to the governments of the Soviet Union, the USA and Great Britain, pertaining to the treacherous activities of the government-in-exile and its minister, Draža Mihailović.

In line with the achievements and results of our Liberation struggle, particularly in 1943 which was a turning point as a result of decisive victories won by the Yugoslav revolution, we could rightfully expect understanding and support from all those who had joined together in the anti-Hitler coalition, and from all democratic and progressive forces. Apart from other things, the Second Session of the AFCNLY had the task of seeing to it that the world learned the truth about the tremendous sacrifices made by our peoples in the struggle for freedom, about their solidarity, in action, with all the enslaved and oppressed, and about their great contribution to the common effort of the Allies in the fight against the forces of the Fascist Axis. Thanks precisely to the Second Session of the AFCNLY, the truth about Yugoslavia began to spread, and the struggle pursued by the peoples of Yugoslavia gained growing support throughout the world.

An untenable parallelism came into being with the establishment of the National Committee for the Liberation of Yugoslavia, as the government of the new Yugoslavia: on the one hand there was the revolutionary government in the country, enjoying no formal international recognition, and on the other the government-in-exile, which still enjoyed international recognition but had no influence with the people. Apart from this, it supported General Draža Mihailović who fought on the side of the occupation troops against the National Liberation forces. Attempts were made to resolve this untenable parallelism at the expense of the independence of the new Yugoslav state as evidenced, for instance, in the proposal that the Yugoslav government be set up on a principle of parity; the National Committee and the government-in-exile, and in the recommendation of the Yalta Conference that the AFCNLY be supplemented by deputies from the Assembly of the Kingdom of Yugoslavia elected in 1938.

Despite such pressure, however, the new people's government, which continued to consolidate thanks to fresh victories in the military and political fields, could no longer be bypassed. Then came Churchill's famous statement in the British Parliament which meant factual recognition of the People's Liberation struggle. The further affirmation of the new state at the international level and the confirmation of its sovereignty and integrity was then fostered by the agreement between the Supreme HQ and Stalin, approved by the National Committee, for Red Army units to enter Yugoslav territory from Bulgaria in the autumn of 1944 for the purpose of engaging in joint operations against the Fascist forces in Southeast Serbia, Vojvodina, and Belgrade; at their own request, Bulgarian units also took part.

Somewhat later, this was followed by an agreement with the reconstructed government-in-exile, with Šubašić as prime minister, which we accepted primarily for reasons of foreign policy. Contrary to the intentions of the reactionaries, the agreement consolidated the international position of the new Yugoslavia and, in the final analysis, the people's government itself. Thus was one more significant victory won.

The decisions passed by the Second Session of the AFC-NLY were a reflection of the strength of the National Liberation movement and the new people's government, the strength of the National Liberation Army. That is why the Second Session of the AFCNLY played a decisive role in the development of the People's Liberation uprising. It made the fighting men believe even more firmly in final victory; it dealt a staggering blow to the maneuvers of the emigré government and Draža Mihailović, and rendered it more difficult for ruling circles in the West to help these traitors.

The Second Session of the AFCNLY gave legal form to the centuries-old aspirations of our peoples to live in a common state of equal peoples.

Comrades, in essence, our revolution reflected the organic link between the genuine interests of the working class, within the framework of each nation and within Yugoslavia as a whole, and the national interests of each individual people. Only if the working class of each nation plays the leading role can independence, equality and independent development be secured, and, on that basis, indestructible brotherhood and unity and firm ties within the federal community.

In other words, the struggle for the rights of peoples, for the affirmation and free, comprehensive development of nationalities, is a component part of the struggle of the working class movement for its progressive revolutionary goals. For, unless the rights of peoples are secured, as our own experience has also demonstrated, there can be no achievement of the goals of the working class movement and the working class, which alone is in a position to secure and to develop continually the Socialist substance of the national interest. Such an approach to national equality simultaneously represents consistent fulfillment of internationalist obligations deriving from the principle of proletarian internationalism. For only a working class movement that struggles consistently for full realization of the rights of peoples can succeed in making a creative contribution to the further advancement of the international workers' movement.

The sovereignty of our Socialist federal community has deep roots in our people's revolution. Our peoples have made enormous sacrifices and spilled rivers of blood to become the masters of their fate, to be able to decide independently on the forms of their socio-economic development, which is also an indispensable prerequisite for broad-based ties and cooperation on a footing of equality, with other countries and peoples. Fighting for their own freedom and against the common enemy, the working class and all the peace-minded forces of the peoples of Yugoslavia implemented, in action, the principle of proletarian internationalism and made a major contribution to the victory over Fascism and the strengthening of the international forces of social progress.

The desire of our peoples for freedom, independence and unobstructed development, from which has emerged the sovereignty of our new state, was common to all the peoples joined together in the anti-Hitler coalition. Even during the war, the principles of sovereignty, integrity and equality, were formulated in the renowned Atlantic Charter. After the termination of the Second World War, after the total collapse of the Fascist Axis, those same principles were elaborated further in the United Nations Charter and adopted by the entire international community. For its part, Socialist Yugoslavia has been governed consistently in its policy by those same principles and will continue to be so governed in the future.

Comrades, this anniversary of jubilee makes it incumbent on us to refer briefly to the path traversed in post-war development. It is our duty to do so above all for the sake of our younger generation which is gradually taking over its historic task and continuing the work we inaugurated. This is all the more necessary as the 25th anniversary of the AFCNLY is being celebrated during a period of decisive efforts to implement our economic and social reform, to build up a Socialist society based on self-management.

During the period immediately following the revolution, it was imperative above all to consolidate its achievements to consolidate the military and political power that had been won and secure a material basis for it, through nationalization, agrarian reform and other measures. In view of our legacy of economic underdevelopment and the widespread devastation caused by the war, these tasks required tremendous effort and self-sacrifice.

The year 1947 was an important turning point in the further development of Yugoslavia on its road to Socialism for that is when the National Assembly passed the First Five Year Plan for the Development of the National Economy, adopted by the working people as an action program which they set about fulfilling with unprecedented enthusiasm. All of Yugoslavia was transformed into a tremendous construction site of new factories, railway lines, electric power plants, housing projects for the working people, and many other things. It would have been impossible to pull the country out of its poverty, backwardness and dependence had we not invested the maximum effort in its industrialization and electrification and later in the advancement of agriculture, all of which were prerequisites for accelerating the Socialist development of the country. The self-abnegation and efforts of the working people were tremendous also for the reason that, at the time, we unexpectedly found ourselves in the position of having to struggle to preserve the independence we had won and to defend our right to pursue an independent path of Socialist development.

On the basis of the characteristics of our revolution—during which the foundations for a democratic Socialist society were laid—of the laws governing it, the experience of the first few years of reconstruction of the devastated land and of planned development, and particularly of our desire to find ways and forms of independent Socialist development which would suit us best, awareness grew in this country of the need to put into practice Marx's idea that the factories should be turned over to the workers to manage and that such a socio-economic system should be created in which self-management would be practiced directly by millions of people. In this respect, our point of departure was the fact that the subject of Socialist development could not be the state apparatus, but rather the working class and all working people, associated in their management of the socialized means of production.

By turning the enterprises over to the working collectives to manage, we took the first step towards the creation of such social and material conditions as would make it permanently impossible for bureaucratic relationships to grow, and laid the foundations for development of a self-managing system in this country. We were convinced, and practice later confirmed this, that this was the way for the creative role of the working class and all working people to assert itself and at the same time represented a guarantee that their real interests would be pursued. This was also a reflection of the democratic and humane character of our revolution, in its continuity, in view of the fact that, since the very beginning, man had been in the foreground, and that there had never prevailed in this country the attitude that his interests should be subordinated to some sort of "loftier goals."

The strengthening of society's material base was paralleled by development of the system of self-management and a constant growth in the role of the working man in decision-making on the conditions and fruits of his labor. The working man, as the creator of the surplus-product, is playing an increasing role in deciding how it will be used. Each step taken in the direction of strengthening the material foundations of self-management in the work organizations and expanding the rights of decision-making has led to the fostering of initiative and greater incentive for the solution of the crucial problems of production and income distribution.

By extending self-management to include all spheres of the life of society and by increasing the working man's influence over decision-making at all levels, from the commune through the republics to the federation, the system of self-management in this country has struck deep roots, become a matter of daily practice and an attribute of millions of working people so that no one will ever be able to sway them from this path.

Assuming that under self-managing Socialism, it is the working people who make the decisions on all essential questions pertaining to the development of society, and in keeping with changes in the position of the economic organizations and in the conduct of the economy generally, the entire socio-political system has been modified and adapted. It was therefore made possible for the direct producers really to participate also in the sphere of political decision-making.

Changes in the political structure have been taking place continually, beginning with 1950, and particularly since the promulgation of the new Constitutional Law of 1953, when the principle of social self-management was legalized as the foundation of the socio-political system. The strengthening of the position of the assemblies, as representative bodies in all socio-political communities, from the communes through the republics to the federation; the introduction of chambers of producers; the emancipation of the economy from operational and direct interference by state agencies; the adjustment of the work of the party and other socio-political organizations to the new conditions and new relationships—all of these promoted the processes of democratization and of eliminating statism. By that very fact, an essential change began to take place in the character and role of the state which, instead of being a force above society, is to a growing extent becoming an instrument in the hands of the working people, associated on a self-managing basis. It goes without saying that this process is unfolding only to the extent that Socialism is becoming a reality and a stable social system.

Of course, the development of self-management and the process of eliminating statism have not proceeded smoothly. There have been dilemmas and resistance. At certain stages, the development of self-management even ground to a halt, as bureaucratic and conservative forces opposed, in various ways, the building up of Socialism on democratic, self-managing foundations. Resistance came from various quarters and resulted from different political conceptions, motives and interests, but common to all of them was lack of confidence in the working class and its creative role. The League of Communists, as the political vanguard of the working class, was successful in surmounting all this resistance and breaking the ground for new forms of social organization aimed at promoting the influence of the working people over political decision-making, from the bottom to the top of our social structure.

The economic and social reform which we inaugurated after the Eighth Congress of the League of Communists dealt a decisive blow to bureaucratic and reactionary conceptions, and removed obstacles to the more rapid development of self-managing relationships. This also marked the beginning of a new and significant phase in the process of emancipating labor and creating a truly democratic Socialist society on the grounds of self-management. Now all forces are trained on the construction of such a self-managing system as will be capable of solving effectively the most highly complex problems of modern economy, by integration, by adopting the most modern technology and, on that basis, by incorporating successfully into the international division of labor.

True, throughout the entire post-war period, the tempo of

our development has been rapid and the rate of economic growth high. It would take us too far afield to enumerate all that we have achieved. By way of illustration, let us mention only a few statistics. Over the past fifteen years, industrial production has shot up by almost five times. The number of employed has doubled. Product exports have more than tripled. In recent years, we have made significant gains in the advancement of agriculture so that, today, for instance, we are meeting our wheat requirements ourselves although until recently we had to import. The most eloquent testimony to the dynamics of our development is the production of electric power which has reached the figure of 20 milliard kWh annually, whereas production in the pre-war Yugoslavia was barely over a milliard. Naturally, this has contributed to a steady rise in the living standard. In a single decade, between 1955 and 1965, the total level of consumption went up by a factor of 2.3, real personal consumption by 2.1, and the social standard by 3.5. Over the past ten years, more than a million flats have been constructed, every fifth flat in the country having been built during this period. Significant achievements have also been recorded in the spheres of health care, education, science, culture and so on.

It is certainly our principal task to continue unabated our efforts to develop the economic base of our society, to increase the national income, so as to be able to invest more in the advancement of various spheres of the life of society and in raising the living standard. We must insure steady promotion of Socialist and self-managing relationships and of efficiency in the social and self-managing system; we must offer incentive to foreign and internal ties and to more rapid integration, socially and production-wise.

Our conception of the role and position of the working man, as a free and independent creator in a self-managing society, also assumes the full freedom and independence of each people and nationality. For the equality of the working man in a self-managing Socialist society is inseparable from equality among peoples in a multi-national community. Under the conditions in this country, national freedom, sovereignty and equality of peoples are being achieved in direct dependence upon the degree of development of self-managing relationships within each nation and in Yugoslavia as a whole. It is only on the grounds of the full emancipation of each people and each nationality that it is possible to create the kind of a community in which everyone will feel equal. And the independence of each one individually, and the equality of all, are the condition upon which our unity hinges and the guarantee of our federal Socialist community's strength. Consequently, under our self-managing Socialist system, the sovereignty of all the peoples is manifested first and, on that basis, the sovereignty and integrity of the Yugoslav Socialist community as a whole can strengthen and develop.

The creation of new Socialist relationships within our country also brings up the question of new forms in relations among nationalities. This is not simply a matter of particular problems connected with the development and improvement of the Socialist system. There are also problems of material relationships, that is, the transcendence of economic underdevelopment. This naturally has important repercussions on the general development of Socialist relationships in this country.

In this respect, we must constantly search for principled solutions to the existing problems so as to find the best possible way of pursuing the Socialist interests of both the developed and the less developed.

Despite the tremendous results achieved in the economic development of Yugoslavia as a whole, particularly over the past ten years or so, it will be indispensable to go on solving these problems, as upon this hinges the suppression of all possible kinds of manifestations of nationalism and chauvinism in this country. Solution of this problem must receive appropriate attention in internal policy also for the reason that the question of relations between the developed and the less developed is a highly topical one in international relations as well.

It is in the light of the foregoing that we must conceive of the significance of the most recent proposals relevant to the position and role of the republics and autonomous provinces within the framework of the federation. The transformation of the present Chamber of Nationalities into the fundamental political chamber of the Federal Assembly will make it the basic vehicle of political decision-making and the foundation of mutual negotiation and solidarity, and therefore also of full equality between all peoples and nationalities. Through this kind of decision-making, the federation will affirm itself as a democratic socio-political community of the working people of Yugoslavia. Within its structure there are developing further forms of direct integration of social self-management, which also means integration of all socio-political communities. Such mutual relationships among the socio-political communities, grounded in the common interest, equality and mutual trust also provide the basis for the unity of the Socialist socio-political system, the foundations of which are brotherhood and unity and the determination of all peoples and nationalities to live in the Yugoslav federal Socialist community.

Yugoslavia today is no longer simply a federation of equal peoples. It has emerged into an integral Socialist organism in which there is being developed a specific form of Yugoslav Socialist patriotism, binding all peoples and citizens together with growing power.

Comrades, consistent with the principles upon which we have been building our Socialist community of sovereign and equal peoples, we have also always supported, at the international level, respect for the independence, sovereignty and integrity of other countries. In other words, our foreign policy has ever been an adequate reflection of the relationships we have been developing within our own country. And it could not be otherwise. For peoples who have given so much to achieve their own freedom and independence know how to honor those same efforts when they are made by others; they have selflessly offered their support and assistance to all those fighting for freedom and independence, for the right to their own ways of development and participation on a footing of equality in the international community. This we did in the course of the National Liberation War when we proved our internationalism in action. While we ourselves were investing superhuman efforts in the fight against the enemy, we were helping the liberation struggle of other peoples, respecting their sovereign rights.

During the post-war period, as a Socialist country we have felt and feel today that sovereignty under Socialism assumes the full independence and the responsibility of the revolutionary movement in each country for the selection of its own road of socio-economic development in keeping with specific conditions and the requirements of the people. Only such relationships among Socialist countries and Communist parties can promote the strengthening of the international revolutionary workers' and progressive movement generally.

In the revolutionary practice of the building of Socialism, we have been governed by the internationalist principles that the greatest contribution to the cause of Socialism and progress generally can be made above all by proper solution of the national question and staunch struggle in one's own country for the comprehensive development of Socialist relationships and pursuit of the genuine interests of the working people. In any case, those who do not respect their own country and their own people in the first place cannot respect others either.

The Marxist-Leninist concept of internationalism is based

on the independence and full equality of all peoples, as the basic prerequisite for comprehensive cooperation and the forging of links for the purpose of achieving common goals. Internationalist policy is the more consistent, the more it respects full equality and the more it renders possible the comprehensive manifestation of national individuality. Only in that way can the closeting off of nations within their own narrow frameworks, and manifestations of nationalism on that basis, be nipped in the bud.

Today, the whole world knows that Yugoslavia is a sincere champion of international cooperation based on equality, mutual understanding and respect for other countries, regardless of differences in social system or size and population. We have as a consequence succeeded in developing comprehensive cooperation in the political, economic, cultural and other fields with the largest possible number of countries.

Like all other peace-minded peoples, we wish to build up our country in peace and to secure a happier future for the working people. Consequently, our foreign policy activities are directed toward the struggle for peace and peaceable international cooperation. Just as we contributed as much as we could during the war to the victory over Fascism, so have we throughout the post-war period made our contribution to peace, knowing full well that without it there can be no progress or Socialism.

It is for this reason that we view with alarm the serious deterioration in the international situation that has taken place particularly of late. It is especially disturbing that even today in international relations, the principles of the sovereignty and integrity of countries, proclaimed a quarter of a century ago and adopted by all peace-loving mankind, are not being respected. If these principles, which include the fundamental right of each people to be master in its own country, are not respected, new crises and focuses of trouble will arise and there will be no stabilization of international conditions.

As far as Socialist Yugoslavia is concerned, it will continue to fight perseveringly for these principles, together with all other peace-minded countries and progressive forces.

But despite the aggravation of international relations, we are offered encouragement by the fact that the voice of peace-minded and progressive forces is ever more determined in its demand for the preservation of peace, the independence of peoples and states, the elimination of all interference in internal affairs, and the development of comprehensive international cooperation on grounds of equality.

It gives us satisfaction that on this occasion, too, we may stress that among the progressive and peace-minded forces of the world Socialist Yugoslavia plays a prominent role, thanks to the enviable prestige it has won in the world through its struggle for its own freedom and independence, and through its contribution to the fight for peace and progress.

Comrades, in this brief survey, it has been impossible to offer an appropriate picture of the 25 years of existence and development of our Socialist community—the new Yugoslavia. It has been a painstaking process, fraught with myriad difficulties and obstacles, from various quarters and of various types. But our peoples, thanks to their unity, have surmounted all these difficulties and today they may view with pride the results they have achieved. We have created a Yugoslavia that is new in every respect. With new Socialist social relationships. With the national question solved. With the new social system of self-management, focused on man. With great prestige in the world as a peace-minded and independent country. Our revolution was specific—and specific, too, is our road to Socialism.

Index

Africa, 21, 37, 94, 99, 100, 103, 106–107, 132, 133, 137, 138, 144, 147, 165, 167. *See also* Algeria; Angola; Cairo; Colonialism; Congo, The; Developing Nations; Tunisia; Union of South Africa; United Arab Republic.
Agrarian reform, 57–59, 182.
Albania, 23, 45–46, 65.
Algeria, 98, 100, 102–103, 134.
Allied military missions to Yugoslavia, 20, 30, 37.
Allies, 12, 13, 20, 21, 22, 23, 24, 27, 28, 30, 31, 32, 36, 37, 38, 39, 40, 41, 44, 45, 47, 48, 53, 54, 171, 175, 177, 178. *See also* Great Britain; Red Army; Union of Soviet Socialist Republics; United States of America; West, the.
Americans, *see* United States of America.
Angola, 133.
Anti-Fascist Council of People's Liberation (AVNOJ): First Session, 9–13; Second Session, 14–32; Third Session, 35–49; Jubilee Session, 170–191.
Asia, 107, 132, 133, 137, 138, 144, 147, 165, 167. *See also* China, People's Republic of; Indonesia; Japan; Laos; Vietnam; West Irian.
Atlantic Charter, 27, 164, 181.

Atlantic Economic Community, 139.
Atlantic Pact, 128.
Austro-Hungarian Empire, 172.
AVNOJ, *see* Anti-Fascist Council of People's Liberation.

Bačka, 57.
Banovići, 62.
Bari, 37.
Belgium, 101. *See also* Congo, The.
Belgrade, 38, 39, 40, 41, 160, 164, 179.
Belgrade Conference of Nonaligned Countries, 122–150.
Belgrade, New, *see* New Belgrade.
Berlin, 124, 130, 131, 132.
Bihać, 18, 171.
Bizerta, 133.
Bosnia-Herzegovina, 3, 5–6, 16, 17, 21, 22, 36, 39, 42, 43, 44, 57, 81. *See also* Moslems.
Brčko, 62.
British, *see* Great Britain.
Bulgaria, 16, 17, 22, 23, 39, 43, 45, 65, 66–67, 155, 160–163, 179. *See also* Macedonia; Macedonians.
Bureaucracy, 83–86.

Cairo, 24, 30, 32, 37, 164.
Camp David, 97.

193

Central Europe, disengagement in, 112, 128.
Chetniks, 11, 17, 20, 21, 22, 25. *See also* Mihailović, D.
China, People's Republic of, 94, 146.
Churchill, W., 38, 179.
Co-Existence, 96, 99, 109, 114–121, 124, 141, 142, 143, 144, 145, 147, 150, 190–191. *See also* Disarmament; Disengagement; Nonalignment; Noninterference.
Colonialism, 97, 99–107, 124, 132–137, 149. *See also* Africa; Asia; Developing Nations; Latin America; and listings of specific African, Asian, and Latin American nations.
Cominform, 63–76, 89.
Common Market, 157. *See also* West, the.
Communist Party of the Soviet Union, 70, 74, 76. *See also* Cominform.
Communist Party of Yugoslavia, 4, 17, 25, 51, 52, 58, 61, 63–76, 173, 174, 176. *See also* Communists of Yugoslavia, League of.
Communists of Yugoslavia, League of, 155, 185. *See also* Communist Party of Yugoslavia.
Congo, The, 98, 99, 100, 101–102, 135, 145, 146.
Constitution, Yugoslav, 56–58.
Craiova, 45, 160.
Croatia, 3, 5, 16, 17, 19, 22, 30, 36, 42, 178. *See also* Croats.
Croats, 13, 16, 23, 30, 173. *See also* Croatia.
Cuba, 98, 100, 107, 136.
Czechoslovakia, 47, 65, 67, 154, 156, 163, 164, 167.

Dalmatia, 3, 6, 22, 31, 39, 40, 43, 44, 57. *See also* Dalmatians.
Dalmatians, 21. *See also* Dalmatia.
Danube River, 39.
Debar, 23.

Decentralization, *see* Worker's Management.
Developing Nations, 94–95, 124, 139–141, 149. *See also* Africa; Asia; Colonialism; Latin America; and listings of specific African, Asian, and Latin American nations.
Dimitrov, G., 161.
Disarmament, 97, 99, 107–121, 124–130. *See also* Co-Existence; Disengagement; Nonalignment; Noninterference.
Disengagement, in Central Europe, 112, 128. *See also* Co-Existence; Disarmament; Nonalignment; Noninterference.
Drvar, 36.

Egypt, *see* Cairo; United Arab Republic.
Elections, 54.
Engels, F., 71, 72, 74, 76. *See also* Lenin, V. I.; Leninism; Marx, K.; Marxism-Leninism.
England, *see* Great Britain.
Ethnic relationship in Yugoslavia, *see* Nationalities of Yugoslavia, relationship of.

Fascists, *see* Germany, Third Reich.
Five-Year Plan, 59, 62, 63, 91, 182.
Fiume, *see* Rijeka.
France, 47, 102, 128, 133, 134, 167. *See also* Algeria.

Geneva, 97.
Germany, Democratic Republic of, 130–132, 155.
Germany, Federal Republic of, 98, 130–132, 167–168.
Germany, Third Reich, 3–6, 9–13, 15–32, 35–49, 98, 130, 131, 143, 171–176, 178, 181.
Glamoč, 18.
Goebbels, J., 25.
Gornje Vakuf, 21.

Gorski Kotar, 43.
Great Britain, 13, 21, 23, 30, 32, 37, 39, 47, 178, 179. *See also* Allies; West, the.
Great-Serb hegemony, 16, 24, 26, 173. *See also* Nationalities of Yugoslavia, relationship of.
Greece, 23, 38, 141.
Grol, M., 53, 54, 55, 70.

Hebrang, A., 74.
Herzegovina, *see* Bosnia-Herzegovina.
Hitler, A., 129, 131, 160, 161, 171, 178, 181.
Hungary, 16, 17, 44, 47–48, 65, 155.

Indonesia, 135. *See also* West Irian.
Israel, 165.
Istria, 23, 178.
Italy, 16, 17, 21, 22, 23, 30, 31–32, 37, 38, 44, 141, 168.

Jajce, 18, 36, 177, 178.
Japan, 165.

Karavanke Mountains, 40.
Khrushchev, N. S., 111, 124–125.
Kičevo, 23.
King Alexander I, 26. *See also* Royalist government of Yugoslavia.
King Peter II, 24, 26, 37, 51, 56, 174. *See also* Royalist government of Yugoslavia.
Ključ, 18.
Kolašin, 21.
Kordun, 43, 57.
Kosovo-Metohija, 81.
Krajina, 22.
Krupa, 18.

Land Reform, Law on, 57–59.
Laos, 98, 100, 135.
Latin America, 107, 137. *See also* Cuba.

League of Communists of Yugoslavia, 155, 185. *See also* Communist Party of Yugoslavia.
Lenin, V. I., 58–59, 68, 71, 72–73, 74, 76, 80, 84–85. *See also* Engels, F.; Leninism; Marx, K.; Marxism-Leninism.
Leninism, 177. *See also* Engels, F.; Lenin, V. I.; Marx, K.; Marxism-Leninism.
Lika, 44, 57, 81.
Livno, 18.
London, 20, 37.
Lumumba, P., 135. *See also* Congo, The.

Macedonia, 3, 6, 22, 23, 39, 43, 45, 81, 160, 162. *See also* Bulgaria; Macedonians.
Macedonians, 13, 16, 161, 162. *See also* Bulgaria; Macedonia.
MacLean, F., 30.
Malta, 37.
Marx, K., 71, 72, 74, 76, 183. *See also* Engels, F.; Lenin, V. I.; Leninism; Marxism-Leninism.
Marxism-Leninism, 64, 66, 69, 70, 71, 72, 75, 76, 162, 189. *See also* Engels, F.; Lenin, V. I.; Leninism; Marx, K.
Masleša, V., 20.
Middle East, 165.
Mihailović, D., 20, 21, 22, 24, 25, 26, 40, 178, 179, 180. *See also* Chetniks.
Milošević, S., 20.
Monarchy, Yugoslav, *see* Royalist government of Yugoslavia.
Montenegrins, 13. *See also* Montenegro.
Montenegro, 3, 5, 17, 21, 22, 43, 44, 46, 57, 81. *See also* Montenegrins.
Moscow, 23, 30, 38, 46.
Moslems, Yugoslav, 13. *See also* Bosnia-Herzegovina; Kosovo-Metohija.
Mrkonjićgrad, 18.

Mutual Assistance, Friendship, and Economic and Cultural Cooperation, Treaty of, 46.
Mutual Economic Assistance, Council of, 139.

National Liberation Front of Yugoslavia, 176. *See also* People's Front of Yugoslavia.
Nationalities, Chamber of, 188.
Nationalities of Yugoslavia, relationship of, 5, 13, 16, 18, 19, 26, 27, 49, 56, 71, 75, 154, 172, 174–175, 176, 177, 180, 187–188, 191. *See also* Great-Serb hegemony.
Nationalization, 59, 60.
NATO, *see* Atlantic Pact.
Nedić, M., and Nedićites, 16, 22, 24, 25.
Neretva River, 21.
New Belgrade, 63.
Nonalignment, 123–150. *See also* Co-Existence; Disarmament; Disengagement; Noninterference.
Noninterference, principle of, 116, 154, 163–164, 188–191. *See also* Co-Existence; Disarmament; Disengagement; Nonalignment.

Oder-Neisse border, 132.

Paris, 95.
Partisans, 3–6, 9–13, 15–32, 35–49, 51–54, 153, 171–181.
Pavelić, A., 24, 40. *See also* Ustashi.
Peasants, education of as workers, 80–82, 86, 90–91.
People's Front of Yugoslavia, 54, 61, 62, 68. *See also* National Liberation Front of Yugoslavia.
Poland, 46–47, 65, 67, 155.
Portugal, 133.
Pozderac, N., 20.

Red Army, Soviet, 12, 13, 21, 23, 38, 39, 48, 179. *See also* Union of Soviet Socialist Republics.
Rijeka, 178.
Roman Catholic Church, 58.
Royalist government of Yugoslavia, 16, 20, 21, 24, 26, 27, 37, 51, 56, 173–174, 177, 178, 179, 180.
Rumania, 47–48, 65, 67.
Russians, *see* Red Army; Union of Soviet Socialist Republics.

Šamac, 62.
Sandžak, 3, 6, 21, 22, 46, 81.
Sarajevo, 62.
Self-Management, *see* Workers' Management.
Serbia, 3, 5, 16, 17, 21, 22, 38, 39, 43, 57, 179. *See also* Serbs; Great-Serb hegemony.
Serbs, 13, 16, 22, 24, 161. *See also* Serbia; Great-Serb hegemony.
Sicily, 21.
Slavonia, 57.
Slovenes, 13, 16, 23, 173. *See also* Slovenia.
Slovenia, 3, 5, 16, 17, 19, 22, 23, 36, 39, 41, 42, 43, 44, 57, 173, 177, 178. *See also* Slovenes.
Slunj, 18.
Soča River, 40.
Srem, 40.
South Africa, *see* Union of South Africa.
Stalin, J. V., 71, 179.
Stalingrad, 12.
State, withering away of in Yugoslavia, 89.
Šubašić, I., 37, 41, 53, 54, 55, 179.
Šutej, J., 53, 54, 55.
Sweden, 167.
Switzerland, 167.

Terpesev, D., 160, 161.
Todorov, P., 160, 161.
Trade unions, role of, 86–87, 89.

Trotskyism, 71.
Tunisia, 133.
Turkey, 168.

Union of South Africa, 100, 103, 133–134.
Union of Soviet Socialist Republics, 13, 23, 30, 32, 38, 39, 40, 41, 46, 54, 63–76, 89, 111, 119, 124, 129, 149–150, 155, 158, 166, 178. *See also* Red Army.
Unions, trade; see Trade unions, role of.
United Arab Republic, 165.
United Kingdom, *see* Great Britain.
United Nations, 93–121, 128, 133, 134, 136, 138–139, 141, 145–148. *See also* United Nations Charter.
United Nations Charter, 94, 95, 116, 118, 145, 147, 148, 181. *See also* United Nations.
United States of America, 13, 21, 23, 30, 32, 39, 41, 47, 105, 149–150, 166, 178. *See also* Allies; West, the.
UNRRA, 43.

Ustashi, 11, 16, 17, 21, 25, 40. *See also* Pavelić, A.

Velebit, V., 37.
Vietnam, 165.
Vis, 36, 37, 160.
Vojvodina, 3, 6, 16, 57, 179.

West, the, 53, 54, 55, 90, 105, 128–129, 139, 142, 155, 157, 158, 163, 165, 166, 180.
West Irian, 98, 135.
Wilson, M., 30, 38.
Workers' Management, 79–91, 155, 156, 182–188, 191.

Yalta Conference, 41, 179. *See also* Allies.

Zadar, 178.
Zagorje, 57.
Železnik, 63.
Zivkov, T., 160.
Živković, P., 24.
Zlatibor, 163.
Žujović, S., 74.